BV4253 .S83

FROM THE LIBRARY OF
THE INSTITUTE FOR
WORSHIP STUDIES
FLORIDA CAMPUS

Living in a Dying World

Living in a Dying World

Formerly entitled
The City: A Matter of Conscience

By

GEORGE SWEETING

moody press
chicago

© 1972 by
THE MOODY BIBLE INSTITUTE
OF CHICAGO

Library of Congress Catalog Number: 72-77947

ISBN: 0-8024-4942-5

Printed in the United States of America

To
my former churches and beloved members:

Hawthorne Gospel Church, Hawthorne, N. J.
Grace Church, Clifton, N. J.
Madison Avenue Baptist Church, Paterson, N. J.
Moody Memorial Church, Chicago, Ill.

Contents

	PAGE
Is America Dying?	9
How to Rescue Our Cities	19
How to Effectively Share Your Faith	28
What Would D. L. Moody Do If He Were Alive Today?	36
Reviving a Dying World	44
Why I Believe the Bible	53
What Is a Christian?	64
Holding the Ropes in a Dying World	72
Repentance, a Forgotten Doctrine	79
Civil Disobedience—Right or Wrong?	86
God's Great Manhunt	93
How to Start Living All Over Again	100
How to Live Above Worry	106

Is America Dying?

IS AMERICA DYING? A question such as this will probably be dismissed by a majority of Americans as being sensational.

Many would quickly list fantastic accomplishments such as the moon walk, laser rays, or heart transplants, and conclude that our place of greatness is quite secure. The people in the Roman empire had the same sense of satisfaction.

Dr. Robert Strausz-Hupé, author and historian, says, "Within the Roman empire, law and order prevailed, and never (before) did almost everybody 'have it so good' . . . no foreign power could challenge Rome. [He continues,] Why did this . . . civilization decline at all? And why did it decline so rapidly that, within another 100 years, the Roman Empire was plunged irreversibly into anarchy and penury, ravaged by foreign aggressors and doomed to extinction?"

According to Edward Gibbon, in his classic work, *The Decline and Fall of the Roman Empire,* there were five major causes for the decline and fall of the Roman empire.

1. The breakdown of the family and the increase of divorce.
2. The spiraling rise of taxes and extravagant spending.
3. The mounting desire for pleasure and the brutalization of sports.
4. The continual production of armaments to face ever-increasing threats of enemy attacks.
5. The decay of religion into many confusing forms, leaving the people without a uniform faith.

It is very significant that every one of these factors exists in our nation today. Our daily newspapers continually remind us of growing divorce rates, broken homes, delinquency, inflation, taxation, the pleasure boom, the shocking growth of occultism, and weird religions. All of these are a part of our present world; they were also a part of the Roman world.

Let us channel our thoughts into two of these problem areas — family life and the pleasure boom. Speaking of marriage in Roman times, Seneca said, "They divorce in order to remarry. They marry in order to divorce." Marriage had become merely a form of legalized adultery in the Roman world.

In his book, *Rome, Its Rise and Fall*, Philip Van Ness Myers says, "Divorces had multiplied, and the family seemed about to be dissolved. . . . Augustus strove to arrest this downward tendency by edicts and laws in encouragement of marriage and in the restraint of divorces. But the trouble was too deep-seated in the failing moral and religious life of the times to be reached and remedied by any measures of the state."

In the beautiful Garden of Eden, God united Adam and Eve in the first marriage and blessed the first home. Marriage was not instituted just for convenience or conventionality; it was God's plan for the happiness of people.

God designed marriage to be a duet, not a solo. It is intended to be a beautiful partnership, certainly not a tug-of-war. It is a relationship in which two people are either happy or unhappy. It is a spiritual union; it is also a mental and physical union. It is the flowing together of two lives. The Bible says, "They two shall be one flesh;" and yet divorce today is bulldozing our society to ruin.

THE FATHER

Consider the place of the father in the home. In his book, Myers also says, "At the bottom as it were of Roman society and forming its ultimate unit, was the family . . . The typical Roman family consisted of the father . . . and mother, the sons, together with their wives and sons, and the unmarried daughters . . . The most important feature or element of this family group was the authority of the father. [The historian continues,] It would be difficult to overestimate the influence of this group upon the history and destiny of Rome. It was the cradle of at least some of those splendid virtues of the early Romans that contributed to the strength and greatness of Rome, and that helped to give her the dominion of the world."

But, my friend, something happened. The stability of Roman family life didn't last! By the beginning of the second century, Roman fathers, says Myers, had "yielded to the impulse to become far too complacent. Having yielded the habit of controlling their children, they let the children govern them, and took pleasure in bleeding themselves white to gratify the expensive whims of their offspring. The result was that they were succeeded by a generation of idlers and wastrels."

The Bible tells how Eli's sons went wrong, immediately adding, "For I have told him that I will judge his house for ever for the iniquity which he knoweth; because his sons made themselves vile, and he restrained them not" (1 Sa 3:13).

In other words, God's judgment was upon Eli because of his lack of care for his wayward sons. God intended the father to be responsible for the family. Regarding the principles of the law, God's instruction to the Israelites was, "Thou shalt teach them diligently unto thy children, and shalt talk of them when thou sittest in thine house, and when thou walkest by the way, and when thou liest down, and when thou risest up" (Deu 6:7).

The father was meant to be the priest of the home. What does this mean? Simply that the Father is to lead the home in spiritual matters. The husband and father is God's deputy. He is instructed to carry out God's government in the home.

Unfortunately, many fathers fail in this duty. A father commits a colossal sin when he neglects his family's spiritual life.

Jerome Carcopino, in his book *Daily Life in Ancient Rome,* writes, "The fine edge of character had been blunted in the Rome of the second century A.D. The stern face of the traditional father of the family had faded out; instead we see on every hand the flabby face of the son of the house, the eternal spoiled child of society, who has grown accustomed to luxury and lost all sense of discipline."

That sounds a great deal like our present day, doesn't it?

THE CHILDREN

Although the Bible places the greater responsibility for the home on the father, the children also have a part in the success of the family. The apostle Paul, under the direction of the Holy Spirit, wrote, "Children, obey your parents in all things: for this is well pleasing unto the Lord" (Col 3:20). The word *obedience* chills the atmosphere in our day, but let us remember it is God's command. To fail to teach children to obey is cruel. My dear father recognized his privilege and position in our home. He would often say to us six children, "Children, learn to obey the laws of this home, and someday the laws of the school, state, nation, and God will be easy to obey." Jesus obeyed His earthly parents. If Jesus the eternal Son of God was subject to family authority, then surely every child ought to obey his natural father as well as his heavenly Father.

One of the most beautiful pictures of obedience is that of Isaac allowing his father, Abraham, to bind him and place him upon the altar. He could have refused. In his submission he seemed to say, "I will die rather than disobey my father."

In order to learn obedience, at times a child must be punished. The Bible stresses this. "He that spareth his rod hateth his son; but he that loveth him chasteneth him early" (Pr 13:24). "Chasten thy son while there is hope, and let not thy soul spare for his crying" (Pr 19:18).

"Children, obey your parents in the Lord: for this is right" (Eph 6:1). Why obey? Because it is right. For years parents toil for their children. Anxious nights during illness are spent caring for them. Comforts are forfeited and countless sacrifices made. Therefore, as the Bible plainly states, obedience "is right."

THE MOTHER

Today we also see what might be called the rearmament of the battle of the sexes. Roman history reminds us that as the role of the father decreased, the battle of the sexes increased. Upper-class Roman society witnessed a growing number of wives who wanted to be "emancipated."

Historian Carcopino wrote concerning the wife, "Some evaded the duties of maternity for fear of losing their good looks. . . . Some were not content to live their lives by their husband's side."

What does the Bible have to say on this subject? In Ephesians 5:22-23 we read, "Wives, submit yourselves unto your own husbands, as unto the Lord. For the husband is the head of the wife, even as Christ is the head of the church: and he is the saviour of the body." The union of husband and wife is a reflection of the heavenly union of Christ and the church. Christ is the bridegroom, and the saved ones comprise the church, His bride. As Christ loved and ministered to the church, the husband should love and please his wife. As the church in gratitude is subject to Christ, so the wife is to submit to her husband. This submission is not as unto a despot or dictator, but as unto her beloved.

Some have interpreted Paul's words to mean that man is superior. It is not a question of the superiority of either man or woman, for both are superior in their God-appointed places. No woman is more beautiful than the wife who conducts herself according to the Word of God. No man is more gentle than the man who conducts himself according to the Word of God.

Religious and secular authorities agree that for an ideal marriage, the husband should be the breadwinner, while the wife is the keeper of the home.

The wife and mother has a holy calling of God as a homemaker. This calling is superior to all others and never inferior.

The working wife has been singled out by juvenile authorities as a major contributor to the mushrooming incidence of childhood crime. Today, according to the US labor department, there are over twenty-seven million women with children under eighteen, and eleven million of these woman are working.

Working for what, we ask? Undoubtedly, in the case of poorer families, to make ends meet. But increasingly, statisticians tell us, the wife's wages are being used to pay for children's higher education, a color television, a second car, a retirement fund, and vacations.

Titus 2:5 lists some characteristics of the Christian wife. "To be discreet, chaste [or pure], keepers at home, good, obedient to their own husbands, that the word of God be not blasphemed."

The disintegration of the family as the basic unit of our social structure has not come about overnight. It has been a gradual and insidious deterioration — attacking the stability of the home from within.

One visible result of this deterioration has been the confusion of the roles of the sexes. The sexes are already beginning to dress and wear their hair alike. Unisex fashions are becoming the "in" thing in some circles. The new morality, free sex, and the Pill are some of the phrases of our secular press; these things are indications of chaos regarding sex, marriage, and the family.

Many leading specialists who study family life admit that the family is changing profoundly. Some marital "experts" even predict that the very institution of marriage is "obsolete" and on its way out!

In many ways, America is speeding along the same highway Rome traveled and in the same direction. My friend, unless there is a nationwide turning back to God and the Bible, America will also die. May God help us to return to the Word of God and the biblical concept of the family.

Another cause for the collapse of Rome that Edward Gibbon gave was the mounting craze for pleasure and the brutalization of sports. Sociologist Howard Whitman said, "When any nation has become overly pleasure-seeking, history has already begun its epitaph." Few Romans living in the fourth and fifth centuries realized that their pleasure-filled empire was dying. They were too busy having a good time. How does this apply to America today? *Newsweek* magazine projected that in 1972, Americans would spend one-hundred five billion dollars on pleasure. That fantastic amount exceeds our annual defense budget; it's one-tenth of our gross national product.

America rocks from a pleasure explosion. Every week, twelve million golfers vie for tee-off times; nine million tennis players compete across the nets; while four million skiers spend millions of dollars on equipment and resorts. Each year twenty-three million fishermen and hunters search for game in the woodlands of our nation.

Yes, America is at play! The Bible, of course, does not condemn legitimate pleasure; we all enjoy moments of relaxation. Legitimate pleasure and Christianity are certainly compatible. Paul wrote to Timothy that it is God who gives us richly all things to enjoy. There are many leisurely activities that Christians can enjoy.

How do we determine the legitimacy of pleasure? Here is a simple test. Ask yourself this question: "Do these pleasures encourage my spiritual growth, or do they hinder it?" Recall 1 Corinthians 6:12, "All things are lawful unto me, but all things are not expedient." The word *expedient* means "profitable."

That's the key. Do these pleasures build you up or tear you down? This is the heart of the matter. That new fishing boat may be legitimate, but if it hinders you from regular attendance at God's house and subsequent spiritual growth, then it is not profitable. Do your pleasures help or hurt your growth? Do they encourage you or discourage you? Are they spiritually profitable, or are they unprofitable?

Historian Gibbon says, "From the morning to the evening, careless of the sun or of the rain, the spectators, who sometimes numbered 400,000, remained at eager attention . . . The happiness of Rome seemed to hang on the event of a race."

Today in America, spectator sports are a multimillion-dollar business. One professional event overlaps another, and the play-offs continue to proliferate. And yes, Mr. Gibbon, we have our brutalization too. Injuries evidently are becoming more prevalent among professional athletes. A Chicago sportscaster recently said that the Monday morning injury lists are becoming more important than the game results.

Recreation and athletics in themselves, of course, are not wrong. They are necessary for a balanced life and good health. But when a nation seems to have nothing but pleasure as a goal and obsession, that nation is in serious trouble.

Closely related to Rome's sports craze, was its gambling mania. Gambling on sporting events was big business. As it was in ancient Rome, so it is in America today.

On October 29, 1971, in a front-page feature, the *Wall Street Journal* stated that "law enforcement officials say

Is America Dying?

gambling is the underworld's largest revenue producer, grossing over twenty billion dollars annually."

Have you seen any recent entertainment advertisements for plays or movies? Many are lewd and obscene; there is no other way to describe them. Newspapers that editorialize against pornography, at the same time run large advertisements which graphically reveal the degrading subject matter of these shows. Myers makes this further observation concerning the Romans: "Almost from the beginning, the Roman stage was gross, and immorality was one of the main agencies to which must be attributed the undermining of the originally sound moral life of Roman society. So absorbed did the people become in the indecent representations of the stage that they lost all thought and care of the affairs of real life."

Have you noticed the contents of the corner newsstand lately? These displays overflow with pulp magazines that promote perversion, pornography, and violence.

Samuel Dill, writing in *Roman Society in the Last Century of the Western Empire,* said, "Salvianus . . . assures us that Christians were indulging in the madness of the circus and the wantonness of the theatre, when the arms of the Vandals were ringing round the walls, and that the applause of the spectators was mingled with the groans of the dying and the battle-cries of the attackers."

That's the ultimate in escapism. God, through Paul, said that mankind would turn to physical pleasure in the face of judgment. In 2 Timothy 3:1-5 we read, "This know also, that in the last days perilous times shall come. For men shall be lovers of their own selves, covetous, boasters, proud, blasphemers, disobedient to parents, unthankful, unholy, Without natural affection, trucebreakers, false accusers, incontinent, fierce, despisers of those that are good, Traitors, heady, highminded, lovers of pleasure more than lovers of

God; Having a form of godliness, but denying the power thereof: from such turn away."

In recent years we've seen an increase in degeneration, blasphemy, trucebreaking, selfishness, delinquency, and the desire for entertainment. Yes, my friend, America is dying.

Is there a medicine for our malady? Proverbs 14:34 says, "Righteousness exalteth a nation, but sin is a reproach to any people." To you, if you have never received Jesus Christ as Saviour, Jesus said, "Except you repent, you will all likewise perish" (Lk 13:3, NASB). We must turn from self, from carelessness, and from sin. Paul said, "Believe on the Lord Jesus Christ, and thou shalt be saved" (Ac 16:31).

But what about professing Christians? Have we done our best? Of the Syro-Phoenician woman it was said, "She has done what she could." Have I done all that I can do? Have you? The book of Genesis relates that God would have spared Sodom if ten righteous people could have been found. Will God spare our land? The answer seems to depend on you!

How to Rescue Our Cities

THE CITY IS HERE TO STAY. We cannot ignore, deplore, or flee it forever. At the present time 90 percent of the earth's inhabitants live in 5 percent of the earth's area. Within the next century it is claimed that 30 billion people may live in a universal city that covers the globe. Already the United States is a metropolitan society, with at least 60 percent of its population clustered in the cities. Within the urban areas the masses of coming generations will work out their destinies. In the cities the future of America will be decided for better or for worse.

While the population of the cities mounts and continues, many Christians are selling out and moving to the suburbs. For example, one Bible-believing denomination once had five churches within the city limits of a major city. It now has but one. An evangelical withdrawal has been taking place for many years. In fact, we have been running down a road of retreat in other areas. We have seen this as part of a general retreat from the world. We pulled out first to build our own Bible schools, seminaries, and colleges. The body of Christ has further and further estranged itself from our society by developing "separate but equal" facilities in such things as insurance, cruises, entertainment, retirement communities, book clubs, record clubs, and so on. Now, in effect, we are building our own cities.

Evangelical Christians often equate their faith with nice people, blue skies, smiles, and upper-class goals. In rural America the Protestant is dominant; in fact, the *conservative* Protestant is dominant. His attitudes and style of life set the tone for the whole society — the respectable standard — the

American way. But in the city the Protestant is a distinct minority. Jews and Jewish values are influential. Roman Catholics far outnumber Protestants, operate far bigger church programs. By the time you add a sprinkling of multiple small sects from a melting pot of cultures, you come up with one sure thing: in the city the Protestant life-style is not dominant.

This means that the Evangelical who encounters the city does so with considerable culture shock. The conservative Protestant feels uneasy about being a minority. Culture shock gives the feeling of being trapped in a situation you do not fully understand. One writer explains it like this, "A tourist travels through a strange culture protected by the cocoon of his own culture which he takes along with him. All the strange ways strike him as being quaint. He knows he will leave them soon for the security of his well-known and well-loved ways. These quaint attitudes and manners of the foreign then become the topic of conversation and much laughter with the old friends back home. But when he moves into a foreign culture there is no escape back into the familiar. The quaint ways soon lose their quaintness and are despised. There is increasing nostalgia for the old that remembers only the best . . . the quaint are now paying the piper, and if he wants to dance he must do so in their tune."

The majority of Evangelicals have long held an anticity attitude, associating the city with Sodom and Gomorrah, scarlet women, crime, and filth. This antiurban bias has kept us from penetrating three great segments of the world's population: Hindus, Muslims, and modern city dwellers. Somehow we must come to realize this attitude is suicidal to the church of Jesus Christ.

A few months ago I was visiting in one of the smaller cities of the Midwest. A couple greeted me and took me in hand almost immediately. They soon were extending their condolences to me for ministering in the city of Chicago (wicked, wild, and windy). "Dr. Sweeting," they said, "the only sensible solution is to move out." I shuddered inwardly, and then patiently and (I hope) lovingly, told them of God's compassion for our cities.

It seems inconceivable that at this point in the world's history, thousands of Christians still think like this.

WHY MINISTER IN THE URBAN CENTERS?

Why should we minister in the city centers? The churches of the New Testament set the example.

The apostles concentrated their efforts in the throbbing cities of their day. The ministries in those metropolitan areas were life-and-death struggles. The environment was not easy or compatible with the revolutionary new values introduced by the disciples of Christ.

Ephesus, located at the mouth of the Cayster River, was notorious for its luxury and moral looseness. Diana was the chief object of worship, and opposition to the gospel was fierce.

Corinth, with a population of 600,000, was the largest city in Greece. It was an important seaport, a garrison town, and a strategic highway junction. The Corinthians were particularly prone to sexual promiscuity and enjoyed dragging each other off to court over any little difference of opinion. The city seethed with a mass of merchants, philosophers, exsoldiers, and peddlers of vice.

Rome, metropolitan center of the Roman empire, was riddled with perversions, court plots, and murders. Its prosperity and immorality eventually brought about its downfall.

In these centers of life, Christianity took root and flowered throughout the known world. The disciples went neither to the fringes of the towns nor to the tents of the migrants. They saw no future for the gospel in isolation. They moved into the heart of the cities — into the synagogues, the marketplaces, the busy streets.

Today the city and its ways are increasingly setting the pace of our national life. The city has invaded our homes through the mass media and has attracted our youth. Rather than bewail the evil influence of the city and yearn for a Christian rural past that will not return, we rather ought to face with zest the adventure of learning to live Christianity in a city-dominated culture. God did not give His Son because He so loved the little cluster of people in the church, but because He loved the *world,* the adventuring, seeking, reckless world — where the action is.

John Goodwin, formerly with Inter-Varsity, writes, "Much of our drive to build separate but equal facilities (for use by evangelicals) is the desire to forget the war we are in. We can't forget it very well with drunks stumbling over our feet, so we go to 'Christian' hotels. Non-Christians upset us, not so much because they curse and carouse (we have worse sins of our own), but because they remind us of evaded responsibility. From time to time this guilt gets intolerable (down deep we do love Christ), so we mount our chrome-trimmed chargers, and like knights of old, we gallop out of our castles in search of the dragon. We usually find him in jail, or a skid-row mission or other captive audience (even a fraternity) where we can dump our gospel load and get out again with a minimum of personal involvement of time wasted. Then back to the castle we tear, mission completed. With the draw-bridge slammed shut behind us, we sing 'Safe Am I' and settle down again. Often our castle is psychological, but none the less real."

Jesus prayed, "I pray not that thou shouldest take them out of the world;" yet what Christ did not want the Father to do, we ourselves are doing when we withdraw. We try to create a monastic existence in order to avoid temptations and to live a more "godly" life, but this is a foolish underestimation of the devil's wiles and a perversion of the Great Commission.

WHAT ATTITUDES SHOULD WE HAVE?

We need to look at our attitudes concerning both God and the city.

An Attitude of Faith in God. If we are to reach our urban age we need to cultivate an attitude of holy optimism. I am an optimist because of the sovereignty of God. Paul expresses this attitude in several places; for instance, "If God be for us, who can be against us?" (Ro 8:31). And again he exclaims, "Thanks be to God, which giveth us the victory through our Lord Jesus Christ" (1 Co 15:57). Alone we can only be dragged into the mire of the city. The city exposes and bruises and tears us. But much of what the urban culture uncovers in us is sick and needs to be laid before the healing powers of Jesus Christ.

The apostolic church faced mountainous problems with complete confidence in God. "God is able" was their password into pagan territory. Only a fool would have attempted in human strength what they did. Ancient Israel met defeat at Kadesh-Barnea because the people doubted God's ability to see them through. They forgot too soon. The miracle of the Red Sea, the provision of the manna, all faded from their minds, as they considered their own weakness. Problems? Yes, they had problems. We have problems. Each of us faces his own little custom-designed set of temptations and problems. And as we enter the city world, we have individual areas of vulnerability which need to be exposed continually to the help that comes only from the Lord. Every one of us — at our point of greatest weakness — has a magnificent chance to display God's power. "If God be for us, who can be against us?"

True, the more we insert ourselves into the world, the more

we encounter the agents from the headquarters of evil. If we are to go to the world, we cannot hide our eyes and hope the enemy will go away. Here we have to face him and take him on. But we have access to a power greater than Satan. We have Christ in us. He is our hope. When we step out into the city without Him, we are asking to be knocked out. Jesus Christ is the only adequate shield. There is nothing particularly mystical about the spiritual forces at play in the city; they are a very normal part of human experience. Life here is an open battlefield. But we must be optimistic soldiers, following a Captain who wants always to keep us going and to keep us safe.

An Attitude of Love for Our Cities. In addition to our optimism about the sovereignty of God, we Christians need to work out a positive, rather than negative, image of the city. Protestantism has somehow inherited a false perspective which says, "God made the country; man made the city." Even the names of many churches bear this out: Pleasantdale Community Church, Brookside Baptist, Shady Rest Presbyterian, Mountainside Methodist. Sometimes we get so restful we give the impression of a cemetery! We smile and nod and avoid the closeness within our fellowship that discloses flaws and problems and conflicts. The appearance from the outside may very well be one of living in a trance, a dreamworld where life is unreal.

We imply by our retreats that we can find God in nature. And we do need to withdraw occasionally even as Christ did — at the ocean, or the lake, or in the mountains. But we imply by contrast that God has withdrawn from the city and left only a pit of snakes. We picture the city in our minds as a demonic assortment of hippies, prostitutes, junkies, gangsters, pool halls, slums, and vice dens. The city may have started with Cain, but it will climax with Christ. We need to keep in mind that the destiny of the redeemed is a city.

What about the architectural beauty that lies in the old

sections of a city? What about the fascinating ethnic atmosphere? What about the vigorous spirit in the children, who have not yet been crushed by intolerance and greed? What about the beauty of skyscrapers silhouetted at dusk? Or the traffic flowing through a cloverleaf? Or the interesting people walking down the avenue? What about the gold in the mire?

I like the cadence of the jackhammer. I like the sight of a huge crane hoisting steel beams into place. I like the flow of concrete, the clacking of a million heels on finished pavement. I like the feel of sweat, of tears, and flesh. Here is action; here is life. In the crush of multitudes, the power of the living Jesus can still be sensed. Let us not limit our spiritual experience to the Grand Canyon.

An Attitude of Love for All People. The gospel is for all. The gospel never classifies people by race, class, or social standing.

James pictures two men. One man wore a gold ring, and expensive apparel. The other man, obviously poor, arrived in shabby clothes. The shortsighted usher had made class distinctions in his mind before he ever got into this spot. His quick disposal of the problem at hand placed the well-dressed worshiper in an excellent seat, and the poor man was told to sit on the floor or stand up! James teaches that respect of persons is sin (Ja 2:9).

The inclusive gospel cannot be shared by exclusive people. To label people as worthy and unworthy, as good and bad, as acceptable and repulsive is not consistent with the grace of God. Both are thoroughly antichristian. In Jesus Christ there is neither Jew nor Greek, bond nor free, male nor female. Classism and racism are insults to God. Every man, regardless of outward differences, is made in the image of God. God's love included Philemon and Onesimus; Nicodemus and the Samaritan woman. A great church must include all people, regardless of background. In studying the life of

John Wesley, it is interesting to notice that he ministered primarily to the poor. Liberty and equality were taught by Wesley years before the French Revolution. Our attitude must be one of divine love to all people.

An Attitude of Flexibility in Method. The church, particularly in the city, must remain a bulwark of God's saving grace to all. It must unite a redemptive work with the redemptive Word of God. Some months ago I visited an eighteen-year-old in jail. The parole officer asked me to help him secure a suitable job for Sandy, the young man. I talked several times with Sandy about the power of Christ to change his life and also about his resuming his place in society. We found a job, and then he responded to the call of Christ in his life. Then I asked him if this was the first time he had ever heard the gospel. He shocked me by answering, "Oh no, Dr. Sweeting, I've heard it a thousand times. But this is the first time anyone showed me that they cared what happened to me."

People are sick of words. They are dying for a personal demonstration of the love and power of our sovereign Lord. We must demonstrate Christ's love as we unite our actions with our witness. This outreach could take the form of reading classes for the retarded; language help for the immigrant; employment service for the poor; Christian counseling centers for the disturbed; golden-age clubs for the elderly, all with the purpose of bringing people to faith in Jesus Christ.

All these are earthly demonstrations of an eternal faith in the love and grace of our Lord Jesus Christ. When Dwight L. Moody was asked why he had organized the school that later became Moody Bible Institute, he said that besides training students in the knowledge and the use of the Bible and in gospel music, he wanted to train them in everything that will give them access practically to the souls of people, especially the neglected classes.

How to Rescue Our Cities 27

This is in no way an endorsement of the "social gospel". Rather I am pleading for a Christian awareness of the practical day-to-day needs of people, as we share with them what Christ can do. Although we do this on the mission field, we often neglect the neighbors almost at our back door.

The city congregation everywhere must carve out new patterns of ministry — in the slums, among the hippies, in the arenas of commerce, in the seclusion of a high-rise apartment. The church of Jesus Christ must reach behind the walls of steel and concrete to bring the touch of Jesus that can still change water to wine!

Experts tell us that by 1980, 75 percent of America's population will reside in the cities. Apartment housing is the fastest-growing type of shelter for urban Americans — constructed at the rate of 500,000 units per year. The church must create a method of reaching these contemporary, and often unrelated, urban cliff dwellers.

We can experiment. We can try direct mail to individuals who live in the high-rise apartments. We can begin young adult clubs, home Bible study classes, Bible education programs. A family or individual can move into an apartment building and be a "light" shining in darkness, or "salt" flavoring its environment.

Let us be perceptive about the tremendous resource that is buried in the city's people. Together these attitudes can set off an explosion of love that will be the transformation we need.

But, we must *go!* And we must go humbly, ready to learn as well as to teach; ready — if necessary — to lay down our lives.

How to Effectively Share Your Faith

To PHILIP, the evangelist, God's call must have seemed strange. "Arise, and go . . . unto Gaza, which is desert" (Ac 8:26). Philip had just concluded an overwhelmingly successful evangelistic campaign in Samaria. Many men and women were saved, and a great number were baptized in the name of Jesus Christ. Many were delivered of unclean spirits, the palsied and lame were healed, and joy abounded in Samaria.

Following this mighty moving of the Lord, Philip planned to continue his ministry in other Samaritan villages. But God directed him to the desert and to just one man.

Philip's experience gives us many of the most basic principles about witnessing to others concerning Jesus Christ. Here also is a picture of the sovereignty of God and His use of human instruments to reach the lost. This story emphasizes the value of a soul.

When Jesus was on earth He said, "For what shall it profit a man, if he shall gain the whole world, and lose his own soul? Or what shall a man give in exchange for his soul?"

This is clearly the most important starting point in sharing our faith. Unless we see lost men and women eternally faced with either heaven or hell, we will be unmoved by their condition.

Philip was probably a Greek-speaking Jew, a deacon in the early church. He was burdened to reach the unbelievers beyond the borders of Judea and likely was first to go outside the circle of Judaism to preach the gospel. Most of the apostles had determined to give themselves to study and prayer in the Jerusalem church. But Philip, an evangelist, had a heart so full, that he had to share the gospel with men and women in nearby Samaria.

The full heart cannot be silent. One who has experienced a living faith will be strongly moved to share that faith with others. I wonder about you; is this true of your experience? Is your faith that genuine?

This story indicates some of the ways in which God accomplishes His sovereign purposes in reaching out to those He would save. God permitted great persecution in the early church so that these people were scattered abroad in many places (Ac 8:1). Men were trying to put out the light, and all they succeeded in doing was to spill and scatter the oil, and it flamed wherever it flowed. The apostles preached everywhere they went. Persecution helped to spread the gospel.

This story also indicates certain principles which we can learn and use.

BE SENSITIVE TO THE HOLY SPIRIT'S LEADERSHIP

Philip had gone to Samaria and was carrying on a highly successful ministry. Just at that high point in his ministry, God told him to go down to Gaza, a desert place some eighty miles away. Common sense might have dictated otherwise, but the leadership of the Holy Spirit was definite. God was sending His servant Philip from the crowded city to the barren desert, from the masses of people to a single soul. It is a lesson to us; God's ways are not our ways.

Significantly, Philip obeyed the Lord. He had absolute trust in God that His orders were right.

During World War II the North African campaign was slowed down for a time because the enlisted men did not have complete confidence in their officers. The resulting poor morale and fighting were nearly disastrous.

So it can be with God's servants. We need not hesitate to

move forward when it is the will of God. Had Philip relied on what might have seemed like common sense, had he continued his witness where he had been so successful, he would have stayed in Samaria. But God had other plans for him. And it is absolutely vital that we be led of the Holy Spirit in our witnessing.

Philip "arose and went" (Ac 8:27). If you take the first step in faith, the others come easier. We walk by faith and not by sight. Faithfulness to follow today will prepare you for tomorrow.

RECOGNIZE THAT THE GOSPEL IS FOR ALL MANKIND

As Philip journeyed toward Gaza, he came upon a caravan of soldiers and merchants, and in the center, the treasurer of Ethiopia. Here was the man to whom Philip was sent to share the good news.

We are told that this eunuch had been to Jerusalem to worship, so he may have been a Jew who had reached a high place in the government of Ethiopia. Joseph who became a ruler in Egypt, and Daniel in Babylon, are examples of Jews who prospered in a foreign land. But many Bible students believe he was a Gentile who had been converted to Judaism.

As an Ethiopian, he was probably a Negro. The body of Jesus Christ is made up of all races. Classicism and racism are unchristian. He was important, he was rich, and he was religious. Still he was lost. But he was searching the Scriptures for answers, and he was spirtually hungry. As all men, he needed Jesus Christ.

Philip drew near to this man. He had no reservations about the gospel's being relevant to such a man. Philip realized the gospel is for the rich and the poor, the middle class and the outcast, the high and the low.

SHARE YOUR FAITH WITH HOLY ENTHUSIASM

Philip shared his faith with heavenly enthusiasm. He *ran* to this man. Philip had been Spirit-led and Spirit-filled, and he was thrilled with the opportunity to speak to the Ethiopian about Jesus Christ.

We need some of this kind of enthusiasm. Abraham Lincoln once said, "I like to see a man preach like he was fighting bees." We need heavenly enthusiasm.

Often we think of God as having no concern with passing time. We emphasize that with God "a thousand years are as a day" (2 Pe 3:8). But often time drags, and a day *can* seem like a thousand years. I have sat in an intensive care unit with a sick loved one when one night seemed like forever. As God watches the masses of people whom He loves and for whom He died, a day must seem like a thousand years.

Luke 15 pictures the father of the prodigal running to meet the wayward youth. The father was in a hurry to reclaim his lost son.

After the resurrection of Jesus Christ, the angel told Mary, "Go quickly and tell his disciples." The note of urgency and divine haste runs throughout the New Testament.

Time and again in the Acts of the Apostles, we read that men were bold in their preaching of the gospel of Jesus Christ.

A sad, reluctant Christian is an enigma. When the joy of the Lord is our strength, we must say with Peter, "We cannot but speak" what we know and believe.

ESTABLISH A POINT OF CONTACT

Notice the way in which Philip opens his conversation with this Ethiopian eunuch. He noticed the man was reading the Scriptures, so he took a very direct approach. He simply asked, "Understandest thou what thou readest?"

Jesus, too, often used this direct approach. It may have startled this important man to have a stranger come up and ask, "Do you understand what you are reading?" But I believe the Ethiopian readily recognized that Philip could help him. When we are truly led of the Spirit and sensitive to the needs of men, God will care for the response. May we be as "wise as serpents, and harmless as doves" (Mt 10:16). I think God wants us to be tough-minded and tenderhearted.

So the Ethiopian responded, "How can I, except some man should guide me?" (v. 31).

KNOW THE SCRIPTURES

As God's instruments we must be prepared to guide others in their understanding of the Bible. The Christian is exhorted to study and be ready and able to rightly divide the Word of truth.

Do you know how to lead a person to Christ? Can you unfold the meaning of the Scriptures to another?

Notice how wonderfully God worked to pinpoint the Ethiopian's spiritual need. He "just happened" to be reading Isaiah 53. He had been to Jerusalem but was returning home, evidently spiritually unsatisfied. He was searching that great Messianic passage in Isaiah, but he could not understand it.

Had Philip not responded to the Holy Spirit as he did, this man would have returned home in his ignorance. He would not have known of the salvation of Jesus Christ.

Philip immediately entered into the Ethiopian's experience at the point of his need. He read the passage, "He was led as sheep to the slaughter." And to answer the question "To whom does this refer?" Philip "began at the same scripture, and preached unto him Jesus."

I am sure that many other questions were asked and answered in this encounter. Verse 36 indicates this. Evidently

Philip had taken this man right through the gospel story. I am sure he told him of Jesus' birth, His life, His teaching, His suffering, and His death for sinners. Then he must have told him of the resurrection and the new life offered in Jesus Christ, of the Great Commission, and of the need to be baptized.

Then, as they approached a body of water, the man asked, "Here is water. What doth hinder me to be baptized?"

The Ethiopian had confessed his need, and Philip said to him, "If thou believest, . . . thou mayest." So they both went down into the waters of baptism.

Jesus Christ calls for a public profession of our new life in Him. No one is ready to be baptized until he has made an intelligent decision to receive Jesus Christ as Saviour and Lord.

Philip's work was done, and he was taken away again. The Ethiopian went on his way rejoicing. He must have had a new light on his face, a new thrill in his spirit. He was mastered by a new love.

Philip's story is an example to us in many ways.

1. God's ways of working are not always our ways. Romans 8:28 and Isaiah 55:8 point out that God's will may be quite different from ours in a given situation. Surely Philip acknowledged this, as he readily obeyed the Lord to go down to Gaza.
2. God is sovereign in picking His instruments. He is Lord of all His servants, and He leads individuals to those whom He would draw to Himself. Possibly, many other believers were nearer to the scene in Gaza than Philip. After all, he was up in Samaria. But God had His reasons for using Philip.
3. The Holy Spirit's leadership is essential. We must be sensitive to know the leading of the Lord in witnessing, and we must be anxious to obey Him immediately.
4. We must know the Word of God. Men and women hun-

ger for spiritual guidance. The Christian must study the Scriptures in order to guide others to a knowledge of the Lord.

5. Our presentation of the gospel must be adequate to lead a man to saving faith. Philip did not stop with simply interpreting the passage the Ethiopian was reading. He led the man right through to his baptism. This may not always be possible, but we must be able to do this, nevertheless. Too often, we drop a word or answer a spiritual query and then leave the person without further guidance. This is why it is so important that we stay with or follow up people with whom we share the gospel, if at all possible.

6. The Ethiopian's belief was without fear or shame. He openly confessed his faith and was baptized. To be ashamed is a sad experience. It implies carelessness or failure to come to mature faith. Surely no one can be ashamed to confess Christ! It is unthinkable. Hear the words of Joseph Grigg:

> Jesus, and shall it ever be,
> A mortal man ashamed of Thee?
> Ashamed of Thee, whom angels praise,
> Whose glories shine through endless days?
>
> Ashamed of Jesus! sooner far
> Let evening blush to own a star;
> He sheds the beams of light divine
> O'er this benighted soul of mine.
>
> Ashamed of Jesus! that dear Friend
> On whom my hopes of heaven depend!
> No; when I blush, be this my shame,
> That I no more revere His name.
>
> Ashamed of Jesus! yes, I may,
> When I've no guilt to wash away;

No tear to wipe, no good to crave,
No fears to quell, no soul to save.

Ashamed of Jesus,
I never, I never will be;
For Jesus, my Saviour
Is not ashamed of me.

Can you echo these words with your whole heart today?

What Would D. L. Moody Do If He Were Alive Today?

IF D. L. MOODY were alive today, he would jump right into the midst of the action. He was not just involved in a protest movement. He led one. If he were suddenly to appear in Chicago, the newspapers would likely be reporting such activities as this:

"Chicago: Thousands of students, sprawled on the grass of Grant Park last night, listened attentively as evangelist D. L. Moody told them about a new cause. Many remained after the rally to talk with Moody about how they could become part of the movement.

"Moody, looking like an older, more portly version of the student protesters, with his beard and mod nineteenth-century suit, held the attention of the audience as no previous speaker has done. Though not of their age, he talked their language — straightforward, hard-hitting, unequivocal.

"Several hecklers tried to disrupt Moody's talk, but were silenced when he reminded them that the meeting was a free forum where anyone could speak. Since they had already pleaded for their cause, he was entitled to the same opportunity."

The spirit of protest best typifies this decade. Children protest the authority of parents who often preach, "Do as I say, not as I do." Students protest the absolute authority of school administrators; minority groups and the poor protest the lack of power and money that keeps them from becoming integrated into the larger society; laymen and clergy abhor the absence of vitality in the church; people of all ages, classes, and races protest the continued killing in a war that to many seems useless.

What Would D. L. Moody Do If He Were Alive Today?

But protest by itself is not enough. Moody was not merely a protester; he was also a messenger of redemption. He could offer a positive alternative to protest. Because of this, Moody today would probably capture the hearts and imaginations of Americans as he did during his era. Not only would the newspapers be quoting him and writing about him, but hosts of the television interview and talk shows would want him for guest appearances.

Suppose we tuned in to Channel X late one evening to watch a popular, late night talk show.

HOST: Welcome to our program, Mr. Moody. We're certainly glad you could interrupt your busy schedule to talk with us for a few minutes. How does it feel to be back in Chicago? I'm sure you notice a great many changes since you began your work here in the city?

MOODY: Some things have changed; some have stayed the same. There are more buildings, more people, more of the same kinds of problems there always were. People move faster now that they have automobiles. Maybe they move so fast they can't see what's around them. Over in the neighborhood where my school and church are — around LaSalle and Wells — there's a whole street of shops and bars and places where folks can go spend their money. And on one side, there are tall high-rise buildings, where people live who have money to spend. On the other side there are the dark places where little kids grow up, walk around that street, and look at all the pretty things in the windows. They can try to steal them, but they can't buy them. Chicago is pretty much the same underneath the surface. The poor are still poor, and the rich are still rich.

HOST: I understand you got your start working with the poor kids in this neighborhood. In Sunday schools, I think it was. Right?

MOODY: Yes. We sometimes had more than a thousand boys and girls in our Sunday school.

HOST: That's a lot of kids. How did you teach so many?
MOODY: With love. It wouldn't have done any good to have brought that many in, unless they knew they were important. I'd talk to all that I could, and the teachers would all make sure they talked to every boy in their class — just so the boys would know they were loved.
HOST: That's probably what made them *keep* coming, but how did you get them to come the *first* time?
MOODY: I used to go out in the streets and find 'em. A boy who's grown up on the streets won't come to church by himself, you know. Sometimes I'd give oranges and candy if they'd promise to come to Sunday school. Seems to me it makes no difference how people get to where they can hear the gospel, as long as they get there. I wanted those kids to know I was their friend so they'd believe Christ was their Friend.
HOST: Do you think the same technique would work for you today?
MOODY: Why not? You've always got to go out and bring the people in. If they won't come to the church, then you've got to take the church to them. Now, I was walking down the street the other night — you see, Christ's work can't always be done on Sunday morning — and I saw a young girl, about fifteen maybe, just sitting on the store steps — staring straight ahead. I went up to her and asked her what was wrong. And you know, she started to cry and told me about how she had run away from home and how nobody loved her. So I sat and talked with her and told her that Jesus loved her and asked if she wanted to love Him. Sure enough, she did! Then she wanted me to meet her friends, so I went back with her to an old apartment and found a lot of kids sitting around on the floor smoking something that smelled strong and sweet. She said it was pot and that they were trying to get "high." She introduced me as her "guru" and told 'em to listen because I could tell them a lot about love. They listened

too. I said they could get "higher" by taking in Christ's love than by all the things they were trying. I was referring, of course, to heaven.

HOST: Did they believe you?

MOODY: Well, some of them came to church the next day. And Pat — that's the girl — asked if I would go back to her folks with her. She was afraid to go. So we went on the train out to the suburbs, and my, they were glad to see her.

HOST: Did they understand why she had run away?

MOODY: No, they thought she should have been happy. She had everything. She went to a good school, had a room of her own, all the spending money she wanted. She could do just about what she pleased — just as long as she didn't bother them too much. You see her father has just become president of his company, and he has to work very hard; and her mother has a lot of meetings to go to — church meetings, school board meetings, town meetings.

HOST: So Pat had everything but what she really needed?

MOODY: Yes — love. So it's not just the poor kids with problems.

HOST: *Love* seems to be the big word these days — particularly among the hippies and dropouts and draft evaders. Don't you think it's sometimes overdone? There is such a thing as duty — you know, being a soldier is your duty to your country.

MOODY: No sir. Duty never accomplished a great deal. It's a poor way to try to get people to help. People respond to other people. And even an army can fail, if the men don't love their country or commander. I didn't serve with the army during the Civil War. I think my business and God's business is to bring people back together. I was a chaplain, and I helped with the Red Cross. I spent a lot of time talking to wounded boys. It wasn't duty that kept them fighting when they wanted to run away. No, I'm not so sure *duty* is a good word. Jesus Christ's kingdom is built on love, not duty.

HOST: You find lots of clergymen getting involved in the war issue these days — demonstrating setting up draft evasion counseling centers. What do you think about this?

MOODY: I've always made it a point not to take sides in a political argument. That's an area people get all riled up about. If I start getting linked up with one position, then the people who support the other side won't listen to what I have to tell them about Jesus. I don't have time to waste sitting in jail for helping kids burn draft cards. Now, I'll visit 'em in jail and tell 'em about Jesus. That's what I think is important.

HOST: Mr. Moody, it sounds to me as if you're so concerned about preaching Jesus, that you aren't really worried about all the poverty and tension in some areas of the city.

MOODY: Oh no, that's not true. Of course I do feel that once a man has given his life to Christ, he'll be able to work his way out of his situation, no matter how bad it is. Maybe that was a little easier to do a long time ago, though. Now it seems that unskilled workers have a harder time of it. But Christ says to love your neighbor, and that means more than just preaching to him. You can't talk to a person about Jesus if he doesn't believe you really love him. No, what we have to do is to preach the gospel with our hands and feet; it's the acts of kindness and mercy that are important.

You know the parable about the good Samaritan? A man was wounded and nobody stopped to help him but the Samaritan, and he was an enemy. But he didn't stop to ask questions or make sure the wounded man was the right color or religion or had enough money to pay him. He just did what had to be done to keep the man alive. If I really believe Jesus, I will stop to help anyone I see in trouble.

HOST: And if he just needs physical help, you'd give him that without making any attempt to preach? According to the newspapers, you'd just collar a man on the street and ask if he knew Jesus.

MOODY: I guess I did do more of that when I was younger.

It seemed like there was such a short time. But that's not very loving. No, the Samaritan had compassion. He understood. And if we put ourselves in the place of the person who needs help, we can communicate love. The Samaritan went to the wounded man instead of waiting to be asked for help. We've got to be on the lookout for people who need help. But I always tell people about Jesus and give them a chance to trust Him or even to ask questions. That might be the only chance they have to hear.

HOST: Yes, I see. Not all of the churchmen in the city would agree with you. In fact, I've heard some say they think you're a radical and a rabble-rouser. And what about that nickname — "Crazy Moody"?

MOODY: Yes, I've heard that. But I suppose Moses and John the Baptist could have been called rabble-rousers too. John wore sandals and old skins. He stayed out in the desert, and didn't do many things the way folks thought he should. Neither did Jesus, for that matter. The rabbis and priests were always complaining about Him. What would I be able to do for Christ if I just did what everybody else does? I think you've got to be willing to be considered a little mad if you're really going to follow Christ. Of course, some churchmen want things to be done the way they've been done for generations. Some congregations do too. Always sing three hymns, have an hour long sermon and a fifteen-minute prayer. Now I don't think people ought to be bored by the gospel. You've got to make the service move. If you can't say what you've got to say in a short sermon or a short prayer, something's wrong. The other night in a prayer meeting, I had to tell a fellow to stop so somebody else could have a chance to talk to the Lord. People like to sing, too. And they like songs with a little spirit. Nothing's dull about the music the kids are singing now. So why shouldn't they sing lively hymns when they go to church?

HOST: I guess you're right. I never liked to go to church myself, for just those reasons. But a lot of people say that the church service should be dignified and yours is just too casual.

MOODY: Seems to me people ought to feel comfortable in a church meeting. How can you sit and listen to somebody talk about love and not begin to feel something toward the person sitting next to you? I figure I set the tone for the meeting, since I'm the one who's up in front. If I walk in all starched, the people are going to react the same way. A lot of ministers want to feel closer to the people; so they leave off the robes and just talk straight to the congregation instead of preaching at 'em.

HOST: There's also a lot of experimentation going on within the church today. I've noticed you stick pretty much to one way of preaching. What do you think about this search for new forms to make religion meaningful?

MOODY: Well, now, I stick to one method because it works for me. It might not work for somebody else. I tell the fellas in the school not to try to copy anybody's way of preaching. The important thing is to tell the people about Christ.

Some people are good preachers; others aren't. Sometimes a small group is more effective than a big meeting. We used to have mothers' meetings in homes, because they couldn't leave their children. And you see me now at the rallies where the young protesters are. We can't find fault because things aren't done the way they've always been done in the past, or because they aren't done as we think they ought to be done. Why, even my being on this program with you tonight is a new way of preaching the gospel.

HOST: It is?

MOODY: Of course. Just think how many people watch this program who wouldn't ever come to one of my meetings. But now they've heard that Christ loves them.

HOST: I guess you're right. But, Mr. Moody, there is one social problem we haven't talked about. What do you feel your relationship is to the black person?

MOODY: What's my relationship and responsibility to *any* person? The black person is my neighbor as much as the Jewish person or the Scandinavian person. Now, maybe he won't let me tell him about Jesus because he thinks it's a white man's religion. But that doesn't excuse me from figuring out a way to get to speak to him. I'm not sure what it is yet, but I'm looking for it. Maybe it's tutoring children or just helping black students get some training so they can go back and talk to their families.

HOST: And are you doing that?

MOODY: Oh, yes. You know, since I didn't have an education, I feel it's very important that both kids and adults who can't afford school should be able to go. There are a lot of kids, you know, who are dropouts or who've finished high school but can't afford to go to college. They have as much right to learn as the student whose father sends him to Harvard, don't you think? And if the city or the state can't afford to set up special schools, perhaps the Christians should. Then the kids would know they're loved. That's as important as knowledge — maybe more.

HOST: And you're working on this kind of school now?

MOODY: Yes, we're trying to raise money so we can get started. We've found a storefront building we can use right in the neighborhood where we want to begin, but we need money. Maybe the people watching tonight would like to contribute. Just mail your check to —

And so we tune out on the TV show's interview with D. L. Moody. For a nineteenth-century man, he fits very well into the twentieth century. But he may have been ahead of his time. He was a protester whose protests worked. Moody made an impact on the history of America; for his inflexible message was coupled with flexible methods. He could be all things to all men while his message remained unchanged: "Christ loves you; follow Him."

Reviving a Dying World

It appears as though we are living in the closing hours of a dying culture. The beast empires of the prophetic books seem to be moving about the face of the earth.

Many of our world's great cities are threatened by corruption and violence. The dark clouds of war hover dangerously over the Middle East. Hostilities continue in Southeast Asia, and atrocities are committed on the Indian subcontinent. Red China, now a major power, is anxious to display its muscles.

In many places, common sense and reason have been replaced by mob rule. Our universities have become the centers of social anarchy.

The late J. Edgar Hoover said, "We face the twin enemies of crime and communism. Crime and moral decay are eating at us from within. And Communism stands ready to pick up the pieces."

Amid all this, the church of Jesus Christ has adopted the spirit of this age and is apostate. Situation ethics and the "new morality" have been encouraged; and the masses are blinded to God's truth, God's will, and God's redemption. My friend, we need a spiritual awakening.

When Seneca, the Roman philosopher and teacher, warned his day of the weakness of the Roman empire, they laughed at him. To Roman citizens living in the glitter of success, inspired by their magnificent buildings, their tree-lined avenues, their gushing fountains, and triumphant arches, Rome was unbeatable. Rome was the Eternal City.

It seemed absurd to think that war, taxation, crime, race riots, subversion, and apathy would prevail. But Rome fell.

Reviving a Dying World

The impossible happened, and there were at least five specific, definable reasons for the death of that great empire.

And now, all five causes for the fall of Rome are increasingly prominent in our society! Divorce is bulldozing the family to ruin; for every three marriages in the United States, there is one divorce. Taxes are climbing steadily, and inflation continues to eat away at our standard of living. Pleasure is an obsession to the majority of people. In 1970, a total of eighty billion dollars was spent for national defense. Religion is in a state of compromise and sleep. The five fundamental reasons for the fall of Rome are now glaringly evident in our own nation.

Several years ago Roger Babson, newspaper journalist, stated in an article, "The test of a nation *is the growth of its people*. Intellectually and spiritually! Money and so-called prosperity are of very little account! Babylon, Perisa, Greece, Rome, Spain, and France *all had their turn* in being the richest in the world. And the very fact they *had a turn* is significant, because it was just their turn at being great. And then they declined. And instead of saving them, their so-called prosperity proved to be the ruin of them. Our nation is now the richest, but it could easily become a second-class nation and head downward. Money will NOT save us!"

Babson concluded with these powerful words: "Only a sane, spiritual revival which changes the desires of our people will save us! We must be filled with the desire to render service, to seek strength rather than security, to put character ahead of profit!"

That is very upsetting, isn't it? But if we honestly face ourselves and our national condition, then there is hope. We need divine help! We desperately need a revival!

Unfortunately many people seem to have a false idea of what revival is.

First, let me describe what revival is *not*. Revival is not large crowds. All of us have witnessed large religious gatherings where thousands attended, but by no stretching of the definition could this be called revival.

Revival is not great preaching. As a boy, I listened to the great George Truett. I had never heard such preaching, but it was not revival.

Revival is not people being converted. Where genuine revival exists, people usually are converted. But in the true sense of the word, revival is not the salvation of the lost.

Then, what *does* the word *revival* mean? The word *revival* comes from two Latin words: *re,* which means "again," and *vivo,* which means "to live." The literal meaning is "to live again."

Charles Finney, the great evangelist, defined revival as "a new beginning of obedience to God . . . Just as in the case of a converted sinner, the first step is a deep repentance, a breaking down of heart, a getting down in the dust before God, with deep humility and a forsaking of sin."

J. Edwin Orr simply calls revival, "Times of refreshing from the Lord."

Revival in the spiritual realm is to love Jesus Christ in a new and significant way. Revival is to regain spiritual consciousness.

About once a year I come down with a severe head and chest cold. Immediately I phone my doctor. He, in turn, gives me a good prescription, if I act and do what the prescription requires, I'm fine within a few days.

The Bible contains a divine prescription for our crises. It's God's medicine for moral and spiritual sickness. It's found in 2 Chronicles 7:14. "If my people, who are called by my name, shall humble themselves, and pray, and seek my face, and turn from their wicked ways, then will I hear from heaven, and will forgive their sin, and will heal their land."

"If My people will do their part, *then* I will do *My* part." Let's review together the ingredients of God's prescription.

First, tell me, do you know where revival begins? Consider the first phrase, "If my people, who are called by my name." Revival begins with the people of God.

Have you received Jesus Christ as your Saviour? If so, you're God's child. God is your Father, and you're part of God's wonderful family. Revival begins in our lives, your life and mine.

Sometime ago I concluded a study in the book of Jonah. Let me share with you what I discovered. When Jonah repented of his rebellion, his indifference, and his prejudice, then God caused the people of Nineveh to repent. Jonah's biggest problem was Jonah.

The greatest obstacle to the conversion of Nineveh was not to be found *in* Nineveh. It was not the sin and corruption of the Ninevites, although those were great. It was not the graft-ridden police force or corrupt politicians. It was not the false cults and religions. The biggest obstacle to the salvation of Nineveh was found in the heart of a pious, prejudiced man named Jonah. There was no deceitfulness in all of Nineveh like the deceitfulness in Jonah's heart.

Jonah was the key to the salvation of Nineveh. God's people are the *key* to the spiritual climate of our nation and the world. That means that you and I have a big responsibility. Revival starts with God's children — you and me!

God's prescription for revival also begins with a humbling of the individual. Here is what God said: "If my people . . . shall humble themselves." Take a look at this word *humble*. It means "not proud" or "not arrogant, but modest." The message of James 4:6 is powerful, "Wherefore he saith, God resisteth the proud, but giveth grace unto the humble."

Dr. William Culbertson, our former president and chancellor at Moody Bible Institute, would often say to us in chapel, "Walk humbly before God." His life was an example of his words.

Have you ever had to work with someone who really made life difficult for you? He resisted every idea you had and everything you said? He fought you at every turn? Things weren't comfortable, were they? Can you imagine anything as helpless and hopeless as having Almighty God resist you? I wonder, are we a proud people? Brokenness and humility are the first steps in meeting God's prescription: "If my people . . . shall humble themselves." Paul prayed with tears day and night. David Brainerd, suffering a slow, painful death from tuberculosis, interceded for the souls of the American Indians.

Approximately three billion people on our earth need to see the power of God displayed! God tells us that we are the key to our nation's spiritual condition. Revival begins with God's people, with you and me. The theme of our day is the mass man, a day of computers and collectivism. But here we have the individual "Revive *me,* O Lord." Revival warms the life and makes people human.

Self-examination on the part of the Lord's people is imperative. As long as Christians are unbroken, unconcerned, unimpressed, and unforgiving, revival cannot come. We must say with Elihu, "If I have done iniquity, I will do no more" (Job 34:32).

There's another ingredient in God's prescription, and that is prayer. Did you know that world evangelism is totally impossible apart from prayer? Jesus Christ said, "Go ye, therefore, and teach [make disciples] of all nations." But in ourselves, we are not capable of winning *one* person to Christ — let alone the whole world! We are totally inadequate for the task. Yet "with God all things are possible." Jesus Christ didn't assign us a supernatural task to be done in natural power.

That's why we need to pray. Christ told his disciples, "all power is given unto me in heaven and in earth. Go ye, therefore, and teach all nations, baptizing them in the name of the Father, and of the Son, and of the Holy Ghost" (Mt 28:18-19).

You ask, For what shall we pray? Through the prophet Hosea, God said, "Break up your fallow ground, for it is time to seek the LORD" (Ho 10:12). Fallow ground is dry ground, unproductive ground. We need to pray that we might become productive Christians, instruments fit for the Master's use.

Job was a good man, yet he was not released from his captivity until he prayed for his miserable comforters. Prayer has a boomerang effect; it blesses the one who does the praying.

We need to pray for revival in our hearts, in our schools, in our churches, and in this nation. Our prayers should be definite.

We need to pray for complete yieldedness to the Holy Spirit. God through Zechariah said, "Not by might, nor by power, but by my Spirit" (Zec 4:6). Complete dependence upon the Spirit's leadership is the *only* method.

Revival has always found power through prayer. Go back with me through the centuries to A.D. 30. The city is Jerusalem. The evangelist is a bold, untutored fisherman named Peter. The occasion was a Jewish holiday, when Jews and God-fearing Gentiles gathered from all over the known world. Peter powerfully proclaims Jesus Christ. Three thousand people receive Christ that very day. The secret of the harvest was the power of the Holy Spirit activated by the prayers of God's people.

Move on. The year is 1872. The city is London, England, and the evangelist is a relatively unknown YMCA worker from America, D. L. Moody. On a Sunday evening, Moody is preaching in a north London church. He asks those who have decided for Christ to stand. During the last few days, over 400 people have made decisions for Christ. Ultimately thousands came to Christ through the ministry of Moody. What was the cause? God's people were praying.

My friend, God wants to start with you and me. Do you

want Him to revive you? Can you pray, along with others today, "Here I am, Lord. You're the Potter; I'm merely the clay. Begin Your revival in me right now. Change me. Make me useable, and let me aid in bringing revival to our world."

God's formula continues, "And seek my face." To seek God's face isn't a quick "Lord bless me, my wife, and our two children." It demands determination, steadfastness, singleness of heart, and perseverance. John Welch, the Scottish preacher, felt that a day was misspent if he did not spend from eight to ten hours in prayer for the needs of his congregation.

Once when the English writer John Ruskin was trying to complete a book and did not want to be distracted, he published a notice: "John Ruskin is totally engaged in completing a book and therefore unable to answer calls or correspondence. Consider him dead for the next three months."

We need to seek God's face with that kind of determination and perseverance!

The prescription continues, "And turn from their wicked ways." When ancient Israel finally dealt with the sin of Achan, there was victory. For them to turn from what was wrong meant repentance.

When the early church dealt with Ananias and Sapphira (Ac 5), it started to move ahead again.

Repentance is often difficult because many times we're not sensitive to our sin. Sin is smothered and camouflaged in our day. Sin has been driven underground. These days people don't get under conviction. Instead of experiencing repentance and confession, they visit a psychiatrist who says their conduct is the result of having an austere father, or an over protective mother, or that they act the way they do because they didn't get all they wanted in childhood.

Sin has never changed, my friend, and we have to learn to face it openly and honestly. God hates sin!

As long as David continued in sin, he lacked fellowship, power, and the blessing of God. He was a liability rather than an asset. Then, he faced his sin, confessed it, and repented fully. Oh, may God help us to do the same in these days.

Now let me be exceedingly practical. I want to list seven steps to revival.

1. *Develop the desire to know Jesus Christ better.* Develop a holy dissatisfaction. The contented Christian is the sterile Christian. Paul said in substance, "Jesus arrested me on the Damascus road. Now I want to lay hold of all that for which I was arrested by God." Be thoroughly dissatisfied with your spiritual posture.

2. *Pray for a revolutionary change in your life.* I think of Jacob wrestling with God. He wanted blessing. He wouldn't be denied. Throw your entire life into the will of God. Seek God's very best.

3. *Do what you know to do.* If we pray for revival and neglect prayer, that's hypocrisy. To pray for growth and neglect the local church is absolute foolishness. To pray that you'll mature and neglect the Word of God is incongruous. Put yourself in the way of blessing.

4. *Totally repent.* "Create in me a clean heart!" David sobbed. For a whole year David was out of fellowship. But he confessed his sin; he turned from that sin, and then he could sing again; he could write again; he could pray again.

5. *Make the crooked straight.* If you owe a debt, pay it. Or have an understanding with the people you owe. Zacchaeus said, "Lord, the half of my goods I give to the poor; and if I have taken anything from any man by false accusation, I restore him fourfold" (Lk 19:8). As much as possible, make the crooked straight.

6. *Develop a seriousness of purpose.* Keep off the detours. Let nothing deflect the magnetic needle of your calling. If there is anything that is a Trojan horse in our day, it is

the television set. Beware lest it rob you of your passion and your purpose.

7. *Major in majors.* The Christian life requires specialists. Jesus said in effect, "Be a one-eyed man" (cf. Lk 11:34-36). Paul said, "This one thing I do." Too many of us burn up too much energy without engaging in things that bring us nearer to God.

Refuse to rust out. Start sharing your faith. Make yourself available. Back your decision with your time and talent and dollars. Finally, ask God for great faith in Him. Begin to expect great things.

The Greek word for man is *anthropos,* "the up-looking one." We're to look up, but we are also to hook up. James 1:6 says that we are to ask "in faith, nothing wavering. For he that wavereth is like a wave of the sea driven . . . and tossed."

God is saying, "Come alive!" He is saying, "Look up; hook up!" Let's realize there is human responsibility and human opportunity. Let's stir up the gift that God has planted in us and seek the outpouring from heaven that our nation so greatly needs!

Why I Believe the Bible

THE GREAT EVANGELIST George Whitefield once asked a coal miner in Cornwall, England what he believed.

"Oh," said he, "I believe what my church believes."

Whitefield then inquired, "And what does your church believe?"

"Well," he answered, "the church believes what I believe."

Seeing he was getting nowhere, Whitefield then asked, "What do you both believe?"

The coal worker answered, "We both believe the same thing."

This sort of unintelligent faith is pathetic and only perpetuates error. In the Scriptures we are told to "be ready always to give an answer to every man that asketh you a reason of the hope that is in you" (1 Pe 3:15). Each Christian ought to have an intelligent, unshakable confidence in the Bible.

It was my heritage to be born into a home where the Bible was read and believed. As a child I accepted the Bible to be God's Word, simply because my parents trusted it. As I grew older and was subjected to the sophisticated world, my confidence, in the face of science and higher criticism, began to vacillate. Soon I faced the issue, did I believe the Bible to be unique, or was it simply another book?

There are thousands in this world who repudiate the Bible.

Some rebel against any higher authority. Others have turned the world upside down seeking to establish their position. There are those who tell us that God's Word is not consistent with science. I disagree! Surely the God who made this world is not surprised by modern technology. If the Bible is the Word of God, and if God inspired this Book, then it cannot clash with true science, because God knew all truth from the beginning.

There are many reasons why I believe the Bible. Let me present just a few.

1. THE UNITY OF THE BIBLE

It took five hundred years to complete the cathedral of Milan. Empires rose and fell during its erection. But it all fits together so beautifully that it has been called "a poem in stone." How could this be? The answer is obvious, an excellent architect had planned it.

The unity of the Bible requires one mind as its Author. As we review its pages, the plan of an all-controlling, all-directing, supernatural Architect becomes evident. Rather than confusion, chaos, and a mad conglomeration of ideas, harmony prevails from beginning to end.

In 1 Kings 6:7 we read about the building of Solomon's temple. We are told that although it was seven years in building, not a sound of any tool was heard in its erection. Every stone was cut into its proper size and shape long before it reached the place of building. The amazing fact is that everything fitted together beautifully. My friend, a great architect had planned it.

So it is with the Bible. The English Bible is a collection of sixty-six separate books written by some forty different authors. Some of these men lived hundreds of years apart and hundreds of miles distant from one another. Its words were penned by princes and poets, by physicians and philosophers, by priests and publicans, by shepherds and statesmen, by kings and tax collectors. But the marvel is that instead of conflict, we find unity of structure from Genesis to Revelation. Such unity demands a single mind as Author.

Jesus is the Alpha and Omega of the Bible. In the very beginning, after man had disobeyed God, the promise came

Why I Believe the Bible 55

that the seed of the woman would bruise the head of the serpent (Gen 3:15).

From the time that Cain was born, men looked for a man to be the Redeemer. To Abraham the promise was given, "In thy seed shall all the nations of the earth be blessed" (Gen 22:18).

The ceremonial offerings of Leviticus point to Jesus, the eternal and final Offering for sin. Isaiah proclaimed, "His name shall be called Wonderful, Counselor, The Mighty God, The Everlasting Father, The Prince of Peace" (Is 9:6). Micah cried, "But thou, Bethlehem Ephrathah, though thou be little among the thousands of Judah, yet out of thee shall he come forth." (Mic 5:2).

In the New Testament, Matthew begins, "The book of the geneology of Jesus Christ, the son of David, the son of Abraham" (Mt 1:1).

John declares, "These are written, that ye might believe that Jesus is the Christ, the Son of God; and that believing ye might have life through his name" (Jn 20:31).

Paul said, "For I determined not to know any thing among you, except Jesus Christ, and him crucified" (1 Co 2:2).

Coming to the last book of the Bible, John begins, "The Revelation of Jesus Christ" (Rev 1:1).

Beginning with Genesis, the "book of the beginnings," and through every book, the dominant character is Jesus Christ, the Messiah and Saviour.

The Old Testament looks forward to the coming of Christ. The gospels reveal His life, death, resurrection, and ascension. Acts relates the growth of the things Jesus had begun. The epistles tell how the believers in various places advanced spiritually and numerically. Finally, Revelation presents Jesus as Sovereign and triumphant King.

Jean Jacques Rousseau, the French rationalist, said, "I must confess to you that the majesty of the Scriptures astonishes me, the holiness of the evangelists speaks to my heart and has such striking characters of truth, and is, moreover, so perfectly inimitable, that if it had been the invention of men, the inventors would be greater than the greatest heroes." The product demands the Producer to be God.

Second only to the theme of Jesus Christ, is the theme of man's need and God's salvation.

In the book of Genesis we see the results of sin. Adam and Eve chose their own way, which was directly opposed to divine revelation. They sinned against God. One biblical word for "sin" is *hamartia*. It means "a missing of the target." Sin is failure to live up to God's standards. Sin is missing the mark.

The Bible said of the very beginning of humanity, "All flesh had corrupted his way upon the earth" (Gen 6:12). According to King David: "They are all gone aside, they are all together become filthy; there is none that doeth good, no, not one" (Ps 14:3). Isaiah the prophet confessed, "All we like sheep have gone astray; we have turned every one to his own way." (Is 53:6).

Adam and Eve chose their own sinful way, and this brought judgment from God. Their children and their children's children, sinners by birth and by nature, went their own selfish way. Chapter by chapter and book by book we see that man apart from God is a total failure. We do not teach our children to deceive; rather we must teach them not to deceive. We do not teach them to lie! All this comes naturally.

In and of ourselves there is no solution to the sin and evil that control us. Apart from God there is no remedy for man's condition.

Jean Paul Sartre, the French existentialist has said, "There is no exit from the human dilemma."

The need for a spiritual birth is evident to the most casual observer of human nature. Fallen man needs to be restored.

The Bible presents man's condition with uncolored and unvarnished truthfulness. Man needs God!

The constant theme of the entire Bible is man's sin and God's salvation, our inadequacy in contrast to the complete adequacy of God! This Book wastes no words. The Bible says you are separated from God, and that you will be eternally separated from God unless you repent.

2. The Indestructibility of the Bible

Through centuries of change, the Bible remains unchanged and unchangeable. This fact is sufficient to tell us God is the Author.

Jesus said, "Heaven and earth shall pass away, but my words shall not pass away" (Mt 24:35).

The Bible is the most loved Book and also the most hated. It has often been subjected to the fiery furnace of the unbeliever. But it has always risen out of the flames.

Down through the centuries the enemies of God have tried to banish the Bible. Needless to say, they have failed. Travel back over the centuries to the days of Jeremiah. In that day Jehoiakim tried to destroy the Word of God with fire. Immediately the Lord said to Jeremiah, "Take thee again another scroll, and write in it all the former words that were in the first scroll, which Jehoiakim, the king of Judah hath burned" (Jer 36:28). This infidel king sought to throttle God's Word, but all his efforts were in vain. The Bible stands.

There is a remarkable verse found in the book of Isaiah. "The grass withereth, the flower fadeth, but the word of our God shall stand forever" (Is 40:8). The Hebrew word translated here is *yaqum*. The literal meaning is "rises to stand." The picture is of something which is beaten and broken yet rises to stand.

The edicts of Celsus were thrown against the Scriptures, only to fail. Diocletian, the emperor of Rome, voiced his bloody threats and curses to Bible-owning people. As a result many copies of the Bible were burned, and Christians suffered agonizing deaths. Diocletian considered his attack so complete that he erected a monument bearing these Latin words: *Extincto nomene Christianorum* (The name of Christian is extinguished!) What a pronouncement! What an attack! Was he right? The answer is no! Within ten years Constantine succeeded Diocletian. In A.D. 312 Constantine declared himself a Christian. Diocletian was wrong, for the Bible rises to stand! "The grass withereth, the flower fadeth, but the word of our God shall stand forever." The Bible stands.

The Roman church tried to kill the Bible. Adolph Saphir, the Christian historian said, "Rome also persecuted the Scriptures; but chiefly in this way: that instead of being the custodian of Scripture it became the jailor of Scripture, and for many centuries the Word of God was hidden from the people, and legends and traditions of men became the food of the human mind."

Henry V of England considered Bible reading a crime and passed a law saying, "Whosoever is found reading the Scripture shall forfeit his life and land." All his decrees could not shorten the Bible's life by one minute or lighten its weight by one ounce. The Bible stands.

The unbelievers of the eighteenth century mocked the Bible and predicted its death in fifty years. Thomas Paine, author of *The Age of Reason,* said, "I have now gone through a wood with an ax, and felled trees. Here they lie. They will never grow again."

This man tried to blacken the Bible with the ink of infidels. Before he died it is reported that he cried, "God, help me! O Lord, help me! Jesus Christ, help me!" Someone asked if he wished to believe on Christ, and he replied, "I have no wish but to believe on that subject." The Bible stands.

Why I Believe the Bible 59

Voltaire said arrogantly, "Another century and there will not be a Bible on earth." Voltaire is dead but the Bible lives. The Bible stands. Of all books it is the best-selling book year after year.

The Bible is what William E. Gladstone, the great English statesman, called it, "The impregnable rock of Holy Scriptures."

Robert Ingersoll went up and down the land pointing out the "mistakes" of the Scriptures. Ingersoll said, "In twenty-five years the Bible will be a forgotten book." Wrong again, because the Bible stands. The Bible is here to stay.

There is a striking verse in the Old Testament concerning the constancy of the Bible. Psalm 119:89 declares, "Forever, O LORD, thy word is settled in heaven." The word *settled* is the Hebrew word "*notsab*". This literally means "established or fixed." We believe that the Bible in the original manuscripts is but a copy of that which is "fixed" in heaven.

The Bible is the answer to all the ills of the whole world. It warns humanity of the sea of sin, of the rocks of ruin, of the pools of passion, and of the sandbars of Satan. I believe this supernatural Book to be the Word of God, fully inspired. Its pages have not been consumed. Its message has not been corrupted. Its progress has not been curtailed.

To quote the late Dr. A. Z. Conrad,

> Century follows century — There it stands.
> Empires rise and fall and are forgotten — There it stands.
> Dynasty succeeds dynasty — There it stands.
> Kings are crowned and uncrowned — There it stands.
> Emperors decree its extermination — There it stands.
> Despised and torn to pieces — There it stands.
> Storms of hate swirl about it — There it stands.
> Atheists rail against it — There it stands.
> Agnostics smile cynically — There it stands.

Profane prayerless punsters caricature it — There it stands.
Unbelief abandons it — There it stands.
Higher critics deny its claim to inspiration — There it stands.
Thunderbolts of wrath smite it — There it stands.
An anvil that has broken a million hammers — There it stands.
The flames are kindled about it — There it stands.
The arrows of hate are discharged against it — There it stands.
Radicalism rants and raves about it — There it stands.
Fogs of sophistry conceal it temporarily — There it stands.
The tooth of time gnaws but dents it not — There it stands.
Infidels predict its abandonment — There it stands.
Modernism tries to explain it away — There it stands.
Devotees of folly denounce it — There it stands.
It is God's highway to Paradise.
It is the light on the pathway in the darkest night.
It leads business men to integrity and uprightness.
It is the great consoler in bereavement.
It awakens men and women opiated by sin.
It answers every great question of the soul.
It solves every great problem of life.
It is a fortress often attacked but never failing.
Its wisdom is commanding and its logic convincing.
Salvation is its watchword. Eternal life its goal.
It punctures all pretense.
It is forward-looking, outward-looking, and upward-looking.
It outlives, outlifts, outloves, outreaches, outranks, outruns all other books.
Trust it, love it, obey it, and Eternal Life is yours."

This Book stands like a million mountains seemingly unaware of all the attacks of the enemy. This is another important reason why I know the Bible is the Word of God.

3. The Influence of the Bible upon Men

On Daniel Webster's grave you may read this testimony: "Philosophical argument has sometimes shaken my reason for the faith that was in me: but my heart has always assured me that the Gospel of Jesus Christ must be a reality." Only the Bible has the answer to the needs of the soul.

The Bible does not need to be defended. No one has to prove that the sun shines, the stars twinkle, the moon beams, or that flowers have fragrance. The life-changing results of the Bible speak forcefully of the heavenly Author.

In a Southern state, a number of business and professional men became interested in placing portions of the Bible in parked cars, each portion bearing the name and address of the sponsor. One of these portions was left in a taxicab. Several days later a young man came to the office of one of the men. With great emotion, he took the gospel from his pocket and said, "See this little book? It is not a checkbook, and you see it is not a revolver; but it saved my life and the life of my family. When I found this book in a taxi, I had a gun in one pocket and a bottle in the other. I was through with everything and everybody. It was going to be wholesale murder for my family and suicide for me. But when I opened this book, the first thing I read was, 'Come unto me, all ye that labor and are heavy laden, and I will give you rest.' A new light began to dawn. I cried out for divine help. I see things differently now, and God is solving my problems one by one. Thank you for what I found in that car." From a slave to sin he was transformed into a son of God.

The Bible has changed the lives of millions of people. It gives peace in the place of pain. It translates sorrow into song. This God-breathed Book is a highway to heaven and a guidebook to God. It is a crutch to the crippled, a refuge to the refugee. It is a lamp to the lost, a library to the learned. It contains the world's greatest poetry, history, letters, and biographies. It is a balm of healing to the bereaved, a beacon light to the beguiled.

How do I know the Bible is the Word of God? My heart, my soul, my mind — all that is within me declares it to be so.

Not only does the Bible change individuals, but it has changed nations. The periods of revival and reform go hand in hand in history. Whenever attention is focused on the Bible, new life results spiritually, physically, intellectually, and economically.

Charles Darwin, in his *Voyage of the Beagle,* tells of the indescribable depravity of the people of Tierra del Fuego. So base were these people that weak words failed to portray their condition. Years later he returned to these islands after missionaries had preached and distributed the Bible. The change in these people was so tremendous that Darwin became a regular donor to the missionary society. From cannibals to Christians. How do I know the Bible is the Word of God? Because this Book, when it is received by people, makes the reader like the Author.

Augustine was a wicked young man who cared not for God. His mother continually asked the Lord to save her wayward son. While on a trip to Rome, he was driven by adverse circumstances to read his Bible. In anguish of soul he cried out for mercy and cleansing. Upon his return home, an evil companion called to him saying, "Why do you run away, Augustine? It is I."

He called back, "I run because I am not I." Augustine was a new man because of the Bible.

A pious priest, Martin Luther tried by penance and pain to gain forgiveness, but all to no avail. In one letter, he despairingly exclaimed, "Oh my sin, my sin, my sin!" While reading the Bible in the tower of the monastery at Wittenberg, Luther fully realized, "The just shall live by faith" (Ro 1:17), and he was changed from a humble Augustinian monk to an ardent minister of the gospel.

This book is the unchangeable, unshakable, unmistakable Word of God, and you dare not neglect it. Think of it! Not man's word but God's Word! If the Lord came personally to you, would you ignore Him? He has spoken to you in this Book.

This Book says, "It is appointed unto men once to die, but after this the judgment" (Heb 9:27). This Book says, "He that covereth his sins shall not prosper" (Pr 28:13). "The wages of sin is death" (Ro 6:23). "Be sure your sin will find you out" (Num 32:23). "Why call ye me, Lord, Lord, and do not the things which I say?" (Lk 6:46). "If ye love me, keep my commandments" (Jn 14:15). "For God so loved the world, that he gave his only begotten Son, that whosoever believeth in him should not perish, but have everlasting life" (Jn 3:16). "Whosoever was not found written in the book of life was cast into the lake of fire" (Rev 20:15).

Today you stand before the Bible as one stands before a beautiful cathedral. You will never know its glory till you enter. Linger, and you will be lost. Submit, and you will be saved.

What Is a Christian?

THE WORD *Christian* was born in scorn and ridicule. In the city of Antioch of Syria, a city of a million people, the followers of Jesus were first given this nickname. The word appears only three times in the New Testament.

The first use of the word appears in Acts 11:26, "And the disciples were called Christians first in Antioch." The word *Christian* is found again in Acts 26:28: "Then Agrippa said unto Paul, Almost thou persuadest me to be a Christian." The third usage is found in 1 Peter 4:16, "If any man suffer as a Christian, let him not be ashamed, but let him glorify God on this behalf."

To be a Christian in the early centuries was a life-and-death proposition. Christianity was a faith of heroes. To be a Christian often meant facing a pagan arena and wild beasts; it meant the narrow gate, the restricted way, the denial of self, shouldering a cross, and following Jesus Christ.

The word *Christian* is the combination of two words — *Christ* and *man*. When a man is united with Christ, the two form one word, *Christian*. My friend, a Christian is the combination of Christ and *you!* The sinner receives the Saviour and the Saviour receives the sinner. Christianity is Jesus Christ living through you and me.

The word Christian has often been corrupted. It has been misused and misappropriated to cover the entire civilized world. Thousands of people call themselves Christians who have no claim to the name at all. Some say, "All civilized people are Christians." Others suppose this word includes all Gentiles and excludes all Hebrews. To the contrary, there are many splendid people who are Jewish and Christian; and, sad enough, there are millions of Gentiles who are not Christians at all.

The concept of Christianity has become so distorted, that millions do not know the difference between spiritual regeneration and mere religious profession.

Recently, I asked a man, "Are you a Christian?" Somewhat embarrassed, he replied, "Of course, I was born in America."

The story is told of two American sailors marooned on a South Sea island. Fearing the natives, the sailors hid themselves, until one day they heard several of the inhabitants speaking perfect English. In relief, one of the marooned men exclaimed, "We are among Christians!" Unfortunately, he had equated the speaking of English with Christianity.

My friend, no one in his unforgiven state, has the right to say, "I am a Christian." You ask, "But why?" The Bible says, "All have sinned, and come short of the glory of God" (Ro 3:23).

God's justice and holiness demand that the penalty for sin be paid. Jesus, God's Son, voluntarily died to atone for the sins of all mankind. Only as you and I receive Christ in faith, do we have the power or the legal right to say we are children of God. John the apostle put it this way, "But as many as received him, to them gave he power to become the sons of God, even to them that believe on his name" (Jn 1:12). So first of all, a Christian is one who has received Jesus Christ.

Religion is "in" today. The world is full of people who say, "I believe in God" or "I believe in Christ. I believe in the Bible." Often, however, the lives of such people do not correspond with what they claim to believe. Theirs is not a saving faith, but a spurious, paralyzing, dead faith.

The Bible says, "Faith without works is dead" (Ja 2:20), and again, "By their fruits ye shall know them" (Mt 7:20). If there is no difference, no distinction in a person's life, I'm afraid such individuals are in the flesh, and "shall of the flesh reap corruption" (Gal 6:8).

There is not a prisoner in the world who does not believe it is better to be honest. There is not a drunkard who does not believe it is better to be sober. Mere belief does nothing to change the condition. Faith has come to be thought of as a mere acquiescence to the Word of God. This kind of faith is deadening and damning. My friend, you must believe in a way that saves you!

Never forget that the Bible tells us, "The devils also believe and tremble" (Ja 2:19). The difference between head belief and heart belief is the difference between heaven and hell. Any faith that does not change the life of the individual is not a saving faith; it is a deceiving faith.

WHAT A CHRISTIAN IS NOT

I remember well the happiness of my boyhood days. Ours was a godly home. On Sunday, all six children accompanied Mother and Father to church. Our meals were always started with family prayer. We read the Bible as a family. Ours was a Christian home, yet this wonderful inheritance did not automatically bring me salvation. Relationship to the redeemed does not bring redemption. Kinship to Christians cannot make one a Christian. God's salvation is not by natural generation.

In other words, being born into a Christian home does not make one a Christian. In John 1:13 we read, "Who were born, not of blood, nor of the will of the flesh, nor of the will of man, but of God."

John is saying that no one becomes a Christian by virtue of his earthly parents. The blessing of a godly mother and a saintly father is a great heritage, but this does not make one a Christian.

God has no grandchildren! Godly parents may give you a good *push* in the right direction, but salvation is a definite

What Is a Christian? 67

personal choice.

The Jewish people used to say, "We have Abraham as our father," and therefore they thought that they were safe and secure.

The exponents of Nazism boasted of pure "Aryan blood" and talked of a "super race." This, too, is unscriptural. In the Bible the mystery of blood is in the heritage of sin, derived from Adam by natural birth. The mystery of blood is also seen in the salvation purchased by the blood of Christ. John the apostle simply states that no one becomes a Christian through natural birth.

Good works cannot make one a Christian. Again notice John 1:13. John emphasizes, "Nor of the will of the flesh."

The greatest error which prevails today is that salvation is the result of personal effort. Thousands imagine themselves Christian because they seek to keep the golden rule or because they live decent, moral lives. Some rely upon their religious activity or church membership. In direct contrast, the apostle John says, salvation does not come through "the will of the flesh." Salvation is a *gift* and not a demand!

I once asked a faithful church attender if she were a Christian. She quickly answered, "I have taught in the Sunday school for sixteen years."

I commended her and kindly repeated my question, "Are you a Christian?"

She then told me of her efforts in the ladies' missionary society but did not answer my simple question. This lady was depending on her own efforts to earn salvation. If being active in religious work makes one a Christian, she certainly would be one many times over; but the Bible says, "Nor of the will of the flesh."

We cannot climb the ladder of self-effort to heaven. In fact, Jesus Christ came down the ladder of incarnation at Bethlehem to meet us as we are — sinful, guilty, and helpless.

The Bible message is plain. Paul said, "For by grace are

you saved through faith; and that not of yourselves, it is the gift of God — Not of works, lest any man should boast" (Eph 2:8-9). Salvation is not something you do but Someone you receive. Salvation is Someone, Jesus Christ.

It would be easier to tunnel through a mountain with a wooden spoon than to get to heaven by personal effort, character, or morality. God's salvation is a gift and not a demand!

Religious ordinances cannot make one a Christian. The third phrase of John 1:13 is, "Nor of the will of man."

Recently I asked my doctor, "Are you a Christian?" He answered, "I was baptized by Pastor So-and-So some years ago." After further discussion I learned that he was banking everything on the ordinance of baptism rather than upon faith in Christ.

No man, no matter how prominent or how pious, can make you a Christian. The erroneous idea that some religious leader can make one a Christian by some religious act is false and absolutely contrary to the Word of God. No church ordinance, however important, can forgive sin.

A tramp, obviously under the influence of alcohol, approached evangelist D. L. Moody. "Mr. Moody," he said, "you're the man who saved me."

As the great evangelist observed the bearded face, bloodshot eyes, unkempt hair, and torn clothes, he replied, "Yes, it looks as if I did save you. If the Lord had, you wouldn't be in this condition."

Ministers are instruments of God to perform His bidding. As Paul said, "We are laborers together with God" (1 Co 3:9). Never, and I mean never, can any man confer salvation or forgiveness upon another. Forgiveness does not come from a wooden cross nor from a wooden confessional; not from man but from God alone!

There are those who say they cannot believe what they do not understand. In reality we believe much that we do not

What Is a Christian?

understand. No doctor completely understands the marvels of the digestive system. Yet who would say, "I will not eat until I understand the digestive system"?

Who understands the wind? Yet it is real. When we see a boat sailing on the water we say, the wind is blowing. When we see the clouds skip along the horizon, we know there is wind. When we see trees bend and the dust fly, we have proof that there is such a thing as wind.

Jesus said in John 3:8, "The wind bloweth where it listeth, and thou hearest the sound thereof, but canst not tell whence it cometh, and whither it goeth; so is every one that is born of the Spirit."

WHAT A CHRISTIAN IS

When Jesus spoke to Nicodemus He said, "Except a man be born again, he cannot see the kingdom of God" (Jn 3:3). According to Jesus, a Christian is one who has been born again. Spiritual birth is the only way to enter God's family.

The other day my wife and I had watermelon for dessert. What a mystery. A seed is dropped into the ground. It sprouts; and soon there is a vigorous plant which bears several watermelons, each of which is hundreds of times the weight of the original seed. On the outside of each melon there is a beautiful coat of green, then a rind of white, and an enticing core of red with dozens of seeds, each capable of producing additional watermelons. Now, the most brilliant man could not explain the mystery of a common watermelon, but the most ignorant man can sit down and eat it and have a wonderful time.

Have you experienced God's wonderful salvation? A Christian is one who is born of God. It's the combination of Jesus Christ and you. But there's more. A Christian is one who is surrendered to God.

For the apostle Paul, salvation and surrender were simultaneous. Immediately upon believing, he asked, "Lord, what wilt thou have me to do?" (Ac 9:6). Just as Paul wanted to do God's will only, so every Christian should surrender his entire life. Paul called upon all Christians to "yield yourselves unto God" (Ro 6:13).

Adolph Deissman suggested that the word *Christian* means "slave of Christ." And I agree with that. Love serves because of what He has done for us.

In the Old Testament, God promised Abraham that he would be the father of a great nation, with children as numerous as the sands of the sea. But Abraham had no children. His patience ran out and contrary to the life of faith, he fathered a son by Hagar, his wife's helper. This act was of the flesh, representing man's blundering fleshly way rather than God's way. God called upon Abraham to give up Ishmael, and eventually Abraham surrendered his son. Immediately, God intervened and performed a miracle. In her old age, Abraham's wife, Sarah, gave birth to Isaac, a child of faith. And through Isaac has come the Jewish nation.

God calls each one of us to let go of his own solutions to life's problems and accept the way of faith. Don't hang on to anything; yield everything to the Lord.

WHAT A CHRISTIAN DOES

It is a colossal mistake to imagine you can carelessly ramble along in the Christian life. As Samuel Rutherford said, "You will not be carried to heaven lying at ease upon a featherbed." A great leader in the early church, Tertullian, said, "He who fears to suffer cannot be His who suffered."

The call of Christ today is uncompromising. The words of Jesus were so piercing that the hearers tried to kill Him. Too often the Lord of glory is presented as meek and mild rather than high and holy, soft and sentimental instead of steadfast and strong. Artists and poets have portrayed Christ with flowing chestnut hair and feminine features, going about breathing mild benedictions upon everyone. That's false!

What Is a Christian?

Oh, it's true that He went about doing good; but He was firm, and His words were stringent.

True, He was loving and kind; but do not overlook the demands of His call. "Master," cried one man, "I will follow thee wherever thou goest."

Jesus answered the enthusiastic offer with a staggering response, "Foxes have holes, and birds of the air have nests, but the Son of man hath not where to lay his head."

Christ asked another man to follow Him, but he replied, "Lord, permit me first to go bury my father."

Christ's reply struck back. "Let the dead bury their dead; but go thou and preach the kingdom of God."

A third cried, "I will follow thee; but let me first go bid them farewell, who are at home at my house."

Jesus dealt a crushing blow when He said, "No man, having put his hand to the plough, and looking back, is fit for the kingdom of God" (Lk 9:57-62).

My friend, the Christian life is not easy! Jesus never gained disciples under false pretense. He never hid His scars, but rather He said, "Behold my hands and my feet and my side."

C. T. Studd's motto was, "If Jesus Christ be God and died for me, then no sacrifice can be too great for me to make for Him."

From history's pages we learn of a cowardly young soldier in the army of Alexander the Great. Whenever the battle grew hot, the young soldier would retreat. The general's pride was cut because this timid soldier also bore the name "Alexander." One day Alexander the Great sternly addressed him and said, "Stop being a coward, or drop that good name!"

My friend, that is the message for today. It is time for Christians to start living up to the dignity of their name.

It is time for God's people to cast themselves upon the Lord in humility for a spiritual awakening!

Holding the Ropes in a Dying World

HOLD ON. Hold on tight. Easy now! OK, he's hit ground." So the friends of Saul must have whispered, as they stealthily slipped him over the Damascus wall to escape the Jews who sought to kill him.

How did Saul get into this predicament? What brought about this ill-feeling against him? Just a short time before, he had been brilliant in their eyes, extremely religious and ruthless in his attempt to rid the world of the followers of Jesus. Saul had been convinced that Jesus was an imposter and that His followers were heretics. Because Saul felt he was chosen to dispose of this threat to the Jewish belief in the unity of God, he zealously worked to capture and jail or even kill any Christians he could find.

But God Himself captured Saul. He caught him as Saul was going to Damascus to hunt Christians, and Saul went to Damascus a changed man. In fact, he "preached Christ in the synagogues, that he is the Son of God" (Ac 9:20). The people were amazed; some were skeptical; some were as intolerant of Saul as Saul had been of them.

Consequently Saul began to receive the treatment he had been giving out. He became a hunted man. He could no longer safely walk the streets of Damascus, for soldiers were everywhere. What was he to do? Fortunately Saul had friends, believers in Christ, who cared for him. They led him stealthily through the shadows of the city to the Damascus wall. Then, hidden in a large basket, Saul was lowered through a window. The disciples slowly played out the ropes that held the basket, until they heard it thud to the ground, heard Saul crawl quietly out and move away into the darkness. Then they pulled up the basket and went about their business.

WHO WERE THE ROPE-HOLDERS?

We know what happened to Saul after his escape from Damascus, but what became of the disciples who held the ropes? Who were they? Where did they go? What did they do? Why were they willing to risk their lives for someone they may have just barely known?

Who were the rope-holders? Nobody knows. Nothing more is said about them. Their names are never mentioned. They remain unknown to history, unknown to us. But God knows them. And that is enough. Those disciples were truly servants, for they served without recognition.

Too often people will serve as long as they get publicity. They will donate food or clothing to poor starving people — if their names are printed in the church bulletin. They will give money to build buildings — if a plaque on the wall will carry their names.

Jesus said, "Take heed that ye do not your alms before men, to be seen by them; otherwise ye have no reward of your Father, who is in heaven" (Mt 6:1). In fact, He suggested such secrecy that the left hand would not know what the right hand did.

Whether or not the rope-holders knew this injunction, they weren't concerned. They did the job that was required of them, then disappeared. How many Christians do you know who serve in this way? There must be scores of doctors, mechanics, lawyers, janitors, salesclerks, teachers, secretaries, garbage collectors, executives, and homemakers, who go about their business from day to day, serving Christ in their own way, doing what is required of them.

They hold the ropes, perhaps performing services that don't seem particularly Christian — on the surface, anyway.

For example, do you know a mechanic who never overcharges and always has your car ready when it's promised? Or a busy mother who takes care of her neighbor's children once a week so their mother can have a few hours of quiet? These are not Christian acts performed for the public. They are part of a Christian way of life. These people follow in a tradition of rope-holders who steadfastly serve without publicity.

Perhaps the greatest of the unknown servants are parents. Nowadays we read a great deal about the generation gap, about teenagers rebelling against their parents. This is the way it has been throughout history. It is human nature to resist restraint.

Yet many of us are followers of Christ because of our parents. They patiently suffered through our growing up. They loved us in spite of ourselves and continued to love until we were ready to be on our own — until our basket touched the ground. My mother and father certainly did. They prayed for me, wept over me, scolded me, and loved me. I'm sure their faithfulness kept me from wandering too far off the track. I thank God for parents who hold the ropes for their children and expect no reward. They are like the men who held the ropes for Saul. They hang on no matter what the circumstances.

WHEN DID THEY HOLD THE ROPES?

The ropes were held at the appropriate time. The escape had to be made at night, since daylight was as dangerous for the disciples as it was for Saul. But they weren't really safe at night either.

The Bible also warns us that we struggle "against the rulers of the darkness of this world, against spiritual wickedness in high places" (Eph 6:12).

It seems to me it is fairly easy to be a Christian in the daylight, when we can see where we are going and when life is

Holding the Ropes in a Dying World

uncomplicated. But what happens when darkness falls? What do we do when we are not sure which direction to take because the paths are confused? How do we react when life seems to have no point? Is that the time to forget Christ?

Some do. Peter did — for a time, at least. He was right there holding the ropes when Jesus was popular. But when trouble came, Peter denied His Lord. And Peter had been convinced that he would never do such a thing. We probably all feel like Peter at times.

Though most of us have not been in such a crucial position, some Christians are in constant danger. I know of a minister in East Germany who met with a group of young American Christians. The visiting teenagers were dumbfounded when he carefully shut all the windows in his apartment even though the day was stifling. He explained that he was afraid of being overheard in a discussion of Christianity. Though this pastor could have escaped East Germany, he chose to stay with his underground church. He is holding the ropes for his flock who worship Christ in fear for their lives. In some countries the situation is not so different from Saul's.

This is an age of opportunity, an age of excitement, but at the same time an age of terror. We have sent men into space. We have discovered ways of prolonging life. Yet we still do not understand our own world, and we still manufacture implements of war. We produce food that rots in stockpiles while millions of the world's population slowly starve to death. We send missionaries to Africa and India and South America, but our own neighbors in the ghettos and suburbs do not hear words of love from us. It is a dark age masquerading as an age of enlightenment. Where will it end? What can you do? Hold the ropes, my friends. Hang on tight. Don't let go. God has chosen you; the missionaries you pray for count on you; your children count on you; your neighbors need you; your church needs you. Keep holding the ropes in spite of the confusion surrounding us. Saul's friends did not give up. Don't you.

The disciples held on until the basket touched the ground. They didn't drop it halfway because it got heavy or because they got tired. Saul trusted them to hang on until he was on the ground.

Someone has said that the greatest ability is dependability. It didn't take any great ability for the disciples to hold the ropes. They just had to hang on until they were sure Saul was safe.

That's the key. Once you put yourself in a position of becoming a rope-holder, you can't give up. You can't be responsible for everybody, that's true. You'd be exhausted. But you are responsible for certain people.

For some, you may be the only one holding the ropes. What about the widow who lives next door to you? Her children all live out of town; she hasn't many friends. Who is there to care about her? Perhaps you're the only one.

Then there are those high school boys who hang around with your son. Where are their parents? Why are the kids always at your house? Maybe they need an adult friend to care about them.

And how about those men you have lunch with every day, those busy executives? Do they know anybody else who can show them Christ's love, or is it up to you?

No, you can't hold the ropes for everybody. But there are some who are your special province.

Of course, trying to be a rope-holder may be discouraging. You may serve the widow countless dinners and numerous cups of coffee and still have little chance to talk to her about Christ. Just when you think the kids really accept you, they may back away. And your business acquaintances may never want to consider what Christ has to say to them. All your praying, all your active showing of love may seem useless.

But are you looking for a reward? Or are you trying to

serve Christ? Perhaps you won't see results as you serve. Then again, you might. You never know what God is going to do. You never know when your prayer will be answered or how it will be answered.

So keep praying, keep asking, keep seeking, keep knocking — until your basket reaches the ground, until the answer is found. Then you can let go of the ropes.

WHY DID THEY HOLD THE ROPES?

Perhaps the disciples' reason was simple; someone was in trouble and they could help. Those men didn't really know who they were helping to escape. Oh, they knew something about Saul. They knew what he had been and what he had become. But that was all. They knew nothing of his future ministry.

They had no idea he would preach in some of the most important places in their world — Jerusalem, Antioch, Cyprus. They didn't imagine that he would start churches all over Asia, including Corinth and Rome. They didn't dream he would write letters that would become part of the Scripture. To them he was Saul, a believer, their friend. They were not concerned with who he might be or what he might become. They were concerned about doing their job faithfully.

You may not know who's in your basket. When she hid him in a basket, did Moses' mother know her son would deliver his people from slavery? Did D. L. Moody's mother know what he would become? Did the people who helped Jews escape Germany during World War II know what their charges would become? Do you suppose Lee Harvey Oswald's or Sirhan Sirhan's role in history might have been different if someone had been holding the ropes for him?

None of us really knows about the people we carry in our baskets. But we all have someone. And we must be faithful — as Christ is faithful to us. God doesn't give us a bigger task than we can handle. But He expects us to do the job assigned to us. David did his job with a slingshot. Gideon did his with a vase. An unknown woman did hers with a vial of oil.

Are we doing our job? Are we holding the ropes for the people God has given us? Will we hang on until their baskets safely touch ground?

Christ has called us to be servants. He has called us to be rope-holders in a dying world. Let us follow Him.

Repentance, a Forgotten Doctrine

IN 1927, Charles Lindberg became a national hero by flying alone across the Atlantic Ocean. During that historic flight, his plane, "The Spirit of St. Louis," traveled at an altitude of 4,000 feet and at a speed of one hundred miles per hour.

Today, supersonic jets can fly 50,000 feet in the air, and streak across the sky at 1,500 miles per hour.

In 1896, the electronic genius, Marconi, established the first wireless radio transmitter. With this unique invention, he was able to send and receive a signal over a distance of two miles. The age of mass communications was born!

Today, with the development of television satellites, audiences from around the world can simultaneously view an event being televised.

This is an era of unparalleled technological development!

Unfortunately, this rapid change has not resulted in peace for mankind. Millions of people are in a constant struggle, seeking to find peace through change. Each year, in the United States, fifty million people change their place of residence. Statistics tell us that there is now one divorce for every three marriages. Wife-swapping clubs have become commonplace in many of our nation's cities and suburbs. Arrests in narcotics in the state of California have increased by 2,000 times in the past ten years, as young and old alike search for a satisfying change.

Jesus once told a story of a boy who decided to leave his home and family to find happiness. Taking his inheritance from his father, he wandered aimlessly, seeking thrills in a foreign country.

Eventually, finding himself without friends or finances, he

realized his life was a complete failure. At the end of his rope, and in total despair, he decided to repent and to return home and seek forgiveness.

THE NEED FOR REPENTANCE

The Bible tells us that the basic need of every man is the need for spiritual change. In Luke 13:3, Jesus said, "Except ye repent, ye shall all likewise perish." You may try to change your place of residence or your job or mate, you may even change your surroundings; but until you repent of your sins and experience salvation, you will never know lasting peace and happiness.

Repentance is a wonderful thing! Suppose we could sin but were not able to repent. Suppose God would let us fall but would not lift us up. Suppose we were able to wander far away but were unable to return. Suppose God had permitted the one dying thief to mock and curse Him but had not permitted the other to pray for a place in paradise.

It is the message of repentance that makes the gospel story a message of joy. The sinner can be cleansed! The fallen can be lifted! The prodigal can come home! The enslaved can be freed! *You* can be changed!

The call to repentance is a major theme running through the entire New Testament. The message that John the Baptist preached could be summed up in one word, *repent*. John said, "Repent for the kingdom of God is at hand." He challenged the people to face their sin and to turn from it.

In Matthew 3:7, John told the pious, self-righteous people, "You generation of vipers, who hath warned you to flee from the wrath to come? Bring forth, therefore, fruit meet for repentance."

It took tremendous courage for John to preach that message. I have found that most people do not like to be told that they are sinners. Many do not want to repent. This has been called the day of the comfortable pew and the placid pulpit, a time when few are talking about repentance.

John the Baptist was not afraid to talk about repentance! He was not afraid to "tell it like it is." Often he was up to his leather belt in hot water.

On another occasion John courageously pointed his gun-like finger at Herod and said, "You are living with your brother's wife, and you will be punished and suffer damnation unless you repent." What happened to John? He was sent to prison, and later his head was severed from his body! But his words still ring out, "Repent, for the kingdom of heaven is at hand."

Like John, the message of Jesus' disciples was that of repentance. In Mark 6:12 we read that during Jesus' earthly ministry He commissioned the twelve and, "They went out, and preached that men should repent."

After our Lord's death and resurrection, He again sent them forth "that repentance and remission of sins should be preached in His name among all nations."

Peter's message on the day of Pentecost was a message of repentance. Coupling the prophecy of Joel with the promise of the indwelling Holy Spirit, He related how that the Messiah had come and was rejected by the people. As He preached, the Bible says, "Their hearts were moved." They called unto Peter and the other disciples and said, "Men and Brethren, what shall we do?" Peter's answer was very clear. "Repent, and be baptized, every one of you, in the name of Jesus Christ for the remission of sins."

In Acts 17 we find that the apostle Paul also preached the message of repentance. While standing on Mars Hill addressing the intellectuals and philosophers of Athens, Paul declared, "God . . . commandeth all men everywhere to repent, Because He hath appointed a day, in which he will judge the world in righteousness."

He knew that these proud, self-seeking scoffers needed to

change their attitude before they could ever believe. Throughout the Bible we find that man needs repentance.

When Paul stood before King Agrippa, He gave his testimony of salvation and a masterful defense of his conduct. Paul told Agrippa, "I was not disobedient unto the heavenly vision." He had preached "unto them of Damascus, and at Jerusalem, and throughout all the borders of Judea, and then to the Gentiles, that they should repent and turn to God, and do works fit for repentance" (Ac 26:19-20).

Paul was no respector of persons. His message rang out to rich and poor alike. To Jew or Gentile, philosopher or king, Paul preached repentance!

On one occasion, Peter Cartwright, a fearless evangelist of the early nineteenth century, was preaching in Nashville, Tennessee. Awed by no one but God, and afraid of nothing but sin, the two-fisted circuit rider was told that President Andrew Jackson was in the service, and that he should be discreet. "I have great respect for the President," said Cartwright, "but all men need to be restored, and unless our good President repents of his sin, he will be judged by God."

The Bible says that all men need to repent! Even those in high places.

Unfortunately, I have found that a great many people have a false idea of what repentance is. To understand repentance, my friend, you must know what it is not.

WHAT REPENTANCE IS NOT

Repentance is not conviction, although conviction is necessary. In John 16:8 we read that "When he [the Holy Spirit] is come, he will reprove [convict] the world of sin, and of righteousness, and of judgment." A man may be convicted that he is wrong and not repent.

A man will not call for a life preserver until he realizes he is drowning. He will not call for the fire department until he knows the building is on fire. Conviction is necessary but not all who are convicted repent. Repentance is not conviction.

Repentance is not religion! You may be a very religious person and yet never repent of your sins.

In Acts 8 we are told of a man named Simon who heard Philip preach and became a believer. After watching the apostles perform miracles and minister with great power, He asked that he might purchase this power. Peter told him that because he had thought the gift of God could be purchased with money, he would perish with his money. Simon's belief, his religion, had not been founded upon true repentance.

Repentance is not religion!

You may ask, "Was Simon going to hell? I thought he believed." He did believe — with his head, but not with his heart. He was trying to get to heaven head first. Intellectual assent without true submission.

Repentance is not being sorry for sin! The hymnwriter has penned,

> Could my tears forever flow,
> Could my tears no respite know;
> All for sin could not atone,
> Thou must save, and Thou alone.

To be sorry is not sufficient. There is a godly sorrow that worketh repentance, but there is also a sorrow for sin without repentance.

Judas was filled with remorse, but he did not repent toward God. After committing his sin, he went to the high priest and cried out in sorrow, "I have betrayed innocent blood." He was filled with regret, but that is not enough. There is a difference between sorrow and repentance!

There is not an alcoholic who isn't sorry for the heartache he has caused. There is not a prisoner who isn't sorry that he was caught.

Repentance is not making a resolution to do better. Many men who have found themselves in serious trouble have tried to make a deal with God: "God, if You get me out of this trap, I'll become a Christian." "God, if You heal my child I'll go to church; I'll be a better husband, a better father." And yet as soon as the ordeal is passed the promises are forgotten. Repentance is not making resolutions!

WHAT REPENTANCE IS

"What then," you may ask, "is repentance?" If it is not conviction or religion, if it is not sorrow or the making of resolutions, what is it?

D. L. Moody used to say, "Man is born with his back toward God. When he truly repents, he turns right around and faces God. Repentance is a change of mind." It is a change of heart, and it results in a change of action.

Repentance is the change in the life of a sinner, which causes him to turn away from his sin. It is the recognition of my sinfulness and my acknowledging before God that I am as helpless as He declares. A sinner's idea of himself must undergo a radical revolution. He may have a high opinion of his goodness, but he must be brought to the place where he confesses with Job, "I abhor myself and repent in dust and ashes."

Regardless of his self-esteem, the sinner must confess to God, even as David, "I acknowledge my transgressions, and my sin is ever before me."

Though once he may have boasted as the Pharisee, "I thank thee, God, that I am not as other men," he must humble his soul as the publican, who implored, "God, be merciful to me a sinner."

A steady churchgoer perhaps, a conscientious citizen, a loyal employee, a tender husband — he must, nevertheless, lament with Paul, "For I know that in me (that is, in my flesh), dwelleth no good thing; for to will is present with me, but how to perform that which is good I find not" (Ro 7:18).

He must discard all thoughts of his own righteousness and assent to the inspired indictment: "There is none righteous, no, not one. For all have sinned, and come short of the glory of God" (Ro 3:10, 23).

John Wesley taught Greek at Oxford University at the age of twenty-one. He hazarded his life for the gospel in crossing the Atlantic Ocean many times as a missionary. And yet, by his own testimony, he did not know Jesus Christ as his personal Savior until his Aldersgate experience at the age of thirty-eight. He repented of his sin, and for the first time experienced the peace and joy of God's cleansing and forgiveness.

Are you looking for happiness today? Have you, my friend, been searching for a satisfying change in your life? The Bible says you need a spiritual change. Jesus said you need to repent. He was not talking to murderers or thieves, He was talking to good people, the spiritual leaders of His day. No matter where you are, no matter who you are, the message of repentance calls out today.

In 2 Peter 3:9 we read that "The Lord is not slack concerning his promise . . . but is longsuffering . . . not willing that any should perish, but that all should come to repentance."

Won't you come to Him today? Won't you turn around to Jesus Christ and by faith receive Him as your Lord and Saviour?

Civil Disobedience -- Right or Wrong?

VERDICT: John Bunyan, guilty of civil disobedience. The author of *Pilgrim's Progress* had failed to attend the Church of England and had persisted in preaching without proper credentials. Therefore, he was found guilty of breaking the king's good laws. Arrested three times, Bunyan spent thirteen years in jail for such crimes.

VERDICT: Martin Niemöller, guilty of civil disobedience. During World War II, this German pastor stood before Hitler and declared, "God is my Führer." For this crime he was removed from his pulpit and placed in a concentration camp.

VERDICT: Peter and John, guilty of civil disobedience. These radical, unauthorized preachers, after healing a lame man, stirred the people by attributing this miracle to Jesus Christ and the resurrection. Furthermore, Peter boldly accused the religious leaders of being responsible for the crucifixion of Jesus Christ. For such a crime Peter and John were sentenced to jail.

Civil disobedience is nothing new. For centuries Christians have been caught between giving their allegiance to God and obeying the laws of man. Ever since the Jerusalem hierarchy in A.D. 30 desperately tried to silence Peter and John, Christians occasionally have been forced to disobey some of man's orders. Peter and John refused to be silent in the face of a threatened jail sentence. These first preachers of the gospel had received their authority from Jesus Christ Himself; but because they lacked the necessary papers and approval from the authorities of their day, the Jerusalem leaders were determined to stop them.

Peter and John were too irregular. They didn't march to

Civil Disobedience—Right or Wrong?

the beat of the established order of the day. They were transformed nonconformists.

The priests in charge of the temple were disturbed by these men, because they desired things to be done in a certain way. Money changers selling their doves were allowed, but children of God lifting their voices in unrehearsed praise were out of order. Then too, the Sadducees didn't believe in a resurrection, and they were determined to stop anyone preaching about the subject. And miracles — these were stirring people up. All this was dreadfully irregular.

So the apostles were arrested late at night. The authorities knew that if they made their arrest during daylight hours, the public might cry out against them.

But the Word of God cannot be bound. The apostles had unquestionable power behind them. This dismayed the authorities, because the evidence was so incontrovertible. When the lame man stood before them whole, they could not deny that power.

What made the disobedience of the apostles legitimate? Supernatural power caused them to speak. And this same supernatural power should characterize every Christian. The work of the church is ministering to people. We are to find people who are lying at the gate, excluded from our worship; to lift them up; and to make them worshipers of Jesus Christ. The church will convince no one of its right to speak unless it can point to changed lives in men and women. The world wants to see miracles.

One more thing upset the authorities; that was the apostles' persistence. The hierarchy was used to seeing people melt in their presence. These priests even bent the Roman officials to their wills. But this simple boldness of the apostles was shocking. There was only one way to stop them. Forbid them by law to preach. Then if they persisted, they could be jailed.

But the religious leaders forgot that these men lived by a

higher authority. Said Peter, "We will do right in the sight of God."

Yes, there are times when it is right to disobey the laws of men. When civil law opposes God's law, we are obliged to disobey. But there are also times when it is wrong to disobey.

A few examples from the Scripture will illustrate this distinction.

Exodus 1 tells of an Egyptian ruler who ordered the death of every Hebrew male child. But Exodus 1:17 says, "But the midwives feared God, and did not as the king of Egypt commanded them."

Jochebed, the mother of Moses, engaged in civil disobedience when she hid the child in a basket among the reeds in the river.

Consider Daniel 6 and the law of Darius that "whosoever shall ask a petition of any God or man for thirty days . . . he shall be cast into the den of lions."

Daniel, fully aware of this law, disobeyed it. Daniel "went into his house . . . and prayed and gave thanks before his God, as he did aforetime" (Dan 6:10).

Daniel disobeyed the king's law. Daniel was involved in civil disobedience. Jeremiah, too, criticized the government of his time so severely that he was jailed and called a traitor to his nation.

However, there is another side to the question. The Scriptures speak clearly concerning the Christian's responsibility to obey his government.

"Let every soul be subject unto the higher powers. For there is no power but of God: the powers that be are ordained of God" (Ro 13:1).

The apostle Paul is saying that no civil power exists except by God's permission. Therefore, whoever resists civil power resists God's ordinance.

An example is found in Numbers 16, in the story of the

Civil Disobedience—Right or Wrong?

rebellion of Korah and a band of Israelites. The government of the day was a theocracy, and Moses was God's chosen civil leader. When the people rebelled against the authority of Moses, God judged them with sudden death. Jude 11 includes this kind of insurrection in a catalog of the evils of the last days.

1 Peter 2:13 tells us, "Submit yourselves to every ordinance of man for the Lord's sake: whether it be to the king, as supreme."

Now, of course, the problem is to reconcile these apparently paradoxical instructions of Scripture. This is a difficult problem to many Christians today. There are several questions that we should consider:

1. What would you do if you lived in Red China today? Civil law forbids you to gather for religious services. Yet the Bible says, "Forsaking not the assembling of ourselves together."

2. If you lived in Germany during Hitler's time, would you have turned a Jewish neighbor over to the SS Troops, or would you have defied the government and hidden him?

3. If you were a pastor in Russia, would you preach against the atheistic doctrines of communism, or merely teach the sections of Scripture that would not conflict?

4. If you were a believer in Christ living in Cuba, would you join a revolutionary movement to overthrow Fidel Castro?

5. If the US were involved in an unjust war, what would you do as a citizen?

The ultimate test concerns the will of God in these matters. Peter was determined to obey God. He demonstrated that there are times when we must obey God rather than men.

Some guidelines in this area should help us.

1. Disobedience, if necessary, must be without violence. To be violent and to hurt someone is contrary to the teaching of the Word of God. The riots which shake our country

are violent and evil. These things seem to be perpetrated by extremists who have no use for the laws of God.

2. The law being disobeyed must be clearly contrary to the Word of God. This was Peter and John's situation. They were commanded by their Lord to bear witness to the things they had seen and heard. The command of the authorities to be silent was clearly in conflict with God's word to them.

Many young men who are dodging the draft today are disobeying simply because they are self-centered and feel no obligation to serve their country. But others feel that God's Word specifically teaches that Christians should resist military service. For this reason they become pacifists. Each youth must decide these matters in light of the Spirit's teaching in the Word of God. And the laws of the United States provide for honest, conscientious objectors.

3. In general, disobedience must not be against civil rulers, because these rulers (both good ones and bad ones) fall within God's permissive and directive will.

Peter and Paul lived and served while wicked Nero held sway, yet both commanded believers to be submissive to the government. The direct teaching of Scripture requires civil obedience (Ro 13:1-7; 1 Pe 2:13-17).

Henry David Thoreau is often referred to by present-day dissenters. Thoreau stated, "It is not desirable to cultivate a respect for the law, so much as for the right." But, we must ask, who decides what is right? The government may make a mistake, but so may the people. If seven people disobey, that is one thing. But if seven million disobey, that is anarchy.

4. Christians must be willing to bear the consequences which disobedience to civil authority involves. Peter and John were so committed to Jesus Christ that they were willing to suffer ridicule, jail, and death to get out the gospel.

The Scriptures imply that ordinarily the commandments of God and the commandments of men should not be in conflict. But it also establishes that God is the Lord of the Christian's conscience. However, for the most part, *obedience is in* and *disobedience is out.* If we are forbidden to bear witness to salvation in Christ, we must disobey that command. If we are ordered by authorities to do evil in the sight of God, we must disóbey.

But there is so much which can be done without disobeying! We must ask, what is the church willing to do today to get out the gospel? Can we be complacent when the world is in such great need?

Every day this week ten thousand people will die of malnutrition or starvation. More than half the world's population lives in perpetual hunger. Millions more are diseased. The World Health Organization tells us that the number of malaria cases annually exceeds 200 million, with two million people dying of the disease each year.

At the same time, millions of people are racially resentful today. Rev. Max Warren, secretary of a missionary society in Africa writes, "The revulsion of Africa against the money-motivated white man, unless checked, will fill our papers with horror items beside which the Mau Mau crimes will seem like Sunday School tales."

The Christ of the churches is saying to us today, "Because thou art lukewarm, and neither cold nor hot, I will spue thee out of my mouth." There came a time in the life of the Laodicean church when they ceased to be a mission force and they became a mission field.

Has this happened to the church of Christ today? A cozy, friendly church is an incredible contradiction in the face of world need.

Peter and John were men on fire for the sake of the gospel. They preached in the face of every difficulty. They ministered God's Word. They fed the hungry. They cared for the widows. All this for the sake of Christ and the gospel.

May God revive us in these times and make us alert soldiers of the cross.

God's Great Manhunt

OUR NATION was shocked some time ago by the mass murder of eight young student nurses in a Chicago hospital dormitory. Corazon Amurao, an exchange nurse from the Philippines, was the only one to escape. Through police photographs, she was able to identify Richard Speck as the killer. Literally thousands of police were mobilized in a massive manhunt to find this twenty-five-year-old man.

After three days on the run, Speck ended up in the Starr Hotel on West Madison Street. There, in cage 584, an eight-by-six-foot wire cubicle costing ninety cents a night, Speck was found.

Speck had drifted through the underbelly of this great city, reading papers, drinking heavily, and hiding out on skid row. The day before he was captured he had spent drinking, trying to find courage to end his life. At 12:30 A.M. Sunday morning, he was rushed to the Cook County Hospital, bleeding to death, an unknown drifter from skid row.

As Dr. LeRoy Smith washed the blood off his arm, he saw the tattoo, which read, "Born to raise hell." Immediately he realized this was the killer. Within minutes the police arrived, and the manhunt was over.

Manhunts are a common occurrence. The United States' Federal Bureau of Investigation is continually searching for its ten most wanted men. Every major nation in the world has an investigative organization which seeks out criminals.

In a very real sense, modern man is in flight. He wants to live his own life, be his own judge, his own creator, and his own saviour. But the more he makes himself independent, the more lonely and frightened he becomes.

In Luke 19:10 we read, "The Son of man is come to seek . . . that which was lost." This verse speaks of the world's greatest manhunt, God in pursuit of wayward man.

THE OFFENSE

What is the offense that caused this divine manhunt? The Bible tells us that the offense is sin.

You ask, What is sin? Sin is to *miss the mark* of God's standard. It is disobedience or lack of conformity to God's revealed will. It is to go our own way rather than God's way.

The first manhunt in the Bible is presented in Genesis, chapter 3. God placed Adam and Eve in a beautiful garden. We read in Genesis 3:6-9, "And when the woman saw that the tree was good for food, and that it was pleasant to the eyes, and a tree to be desired to make one wise, she took of the fruit thereof, and did eat, and gave also unto her husband with her; and he did eat. And the eyes of them both were opened, and they knew that they were naked; and they sewed fig leaves together, and made themselves aprons. And they heard the voice of the LORD God walking in the garden in the cool of the day: and Adam and his wife hid themselves from the presence of the LORD God among the trees of the garden. And the LORD God called unto Adam, and said unto him, Where art thou?"

The first question of the Bible is, "Adam, where are you?" or Man, where are you?

Adam, what are you running from? Why are you naked and ashamed? Why are you AWOL? Genesis chapter 3, pictures God pursuing man.

The second question of the Bible is, "Where is your brother?" Cain in anger had murdered his brother Abel. Genesis 4:9-10 introduces the second manhunt of the Bible: "And the LORD said unto Cain, Where is Abel, thy brother? And he said, I know not: am I my brother's keeper? And he said, What hast thou done? The voice of thy brother's blood crieth unto me from the ground."

Genesis chapter 4, presents God seeking Cain. Where is your brother? Why have you fallen from fellowship? Why do you keep looking back? Why are you on the run?

The psalmist David was on the run in Psalm 139:7-12. He wrote,

> Whither shall I go from thy Spirit? Or whither shall I flee from thy presence?
> If I ascend up into heaven, thou art there; if I make my bed in hell, behold, thou art there.
> If I take the wings of the morning, and dwell in the uttermost parts of the sea,
> Even there shall thy hand lead me, and thy right hand shall hold me.
> If I say, Surely the darkness shall cover me; even the night shall be light about me.
> Yea, the darkness hideth not from thee, but the night shineth as the day; the darkness and the light are both alike to thee.

David recognized the impossibility of hiding from God. Some people today are seeking to flee from God through the use of drugs. Others are seeking to escape down the road of sensual gratification.

Many marriages are on the rocks because of this flight. From the cradle to the grave man frantically runs, seeking satisfaction in things — only to be totally unsatisfied.

Because of sin, we are separated from God. Because we are separated from God, there is no lasting satisfaction. *Sin* is the offense that occasioned the world's greatest manhunt.

THE OFFENDERS

Consider who is being sought. The Bible says, "The Son of man is come to seek and to save that which was lost" (Lk

19:10). Who is being sought? This point is difficult for many people to understand. The tendency is to apply this to the down-and-outers — the Richard Specks, the Lee Harvey Oswalds, the offenders of society.

The book of Romans presents an accurate, unvarnished picture of humanity. "As it is written, There is none righteous, no not one: There is none that understandeth, there is none that seeketh after God. They are all gone out of the way, they are together become unprofitable; there is none that doeth good, no, not one" (Ro 3:10-12).

Romans 3:23 concludes, "For all have sinned, and come short of the glory of God."

This is God's declaration. Like it or not — all have sinned. Regardless of your religious ideas, all have sinned!

When the communists come to the word *sin* in their dictionary, they have written an archaic word denoting the transgression of a mythical divine law. Such definitions are of no consequence; God says, *"All* have sinned."

"All have sinned and come short." This phrase "come short" indicates a complete lack. When a person becomes financially involved to the point where his debts exceed his cash, he may be forced to declare bankruptcy. The word *bankrupt* is used in Romans 3:23. For all have sinned and are *bankrupt* of the glory of God.

One of the ancient manuscripts uses the word *illiterate* for the phrase "come short." "All have sinned and are illiterate of the glory [knowledge] of God." No matter how nice a person you are, you come short of God's standard.

In our jails we place those who are offenders of society. Some are guilty of murder; some have committed theft or forgery, some perjury or slander. Some are violent offenders, some are lesser offenders, but all are offenders. God views mankind and concludes, "All have sinned."

The Bible says, "Whosoever shall keep the whole law, and yet offend in one point, he is guilty of all" (Ja 2:10).

In the eyes of a holy, perfect, God, all mankind is guilty. The apostle Paul writes, "For as by one man's disobedience many were made sinners, so by the obedience of one shall many be made righteous (Ro 5:19). In Adam all are sinful. In Jesus Christ, the last Adam, all can find forgiveness of sins.

If mankind is in flight, there must be a pursuer. If mankind is on the run, someone must be doing the chasing.

THE SEEKER

Briefly, consider who *is doing the seeking.* In the gospel of Luke we read, "The Son of man is come to seek and to save that which was lost." Who is the Son of man? Luke tells us that this one is Jesus Christ.

Seneca, the Roman philosopher, lamented, "If only a hand would reach down to lift me out of my sin." Thank God a hand *has* reached down to us, in the person of Jesus Christ.

God expressed himself on our behalf at Bethlehem. The eternal Word was made flesh. The infinite God became an infant and was born in a manger.

Two Bible words describe the condition of all mankind before God: *dead* and *lost.*

Dead things cannot grow. No one is so helpless as one who is dead. God says, all mankind is dead spiritually and therefore helpless.

Lost is a descriptive word. We are lost like a sheep, separated from the shepherd.

Luke tells of a shepherd with one hundred sheep, but one was lost. The lost sheep could not find her way back to the fold. So the shepherd *sought the lost sheep* and found her. And when he had found her he exclaimed, "Rejoice with me; for I have found my sheep which was lost" (Lk 15:6).

Samuel Coleridge, the great English poet-philosopher, confessed, "I am a fallen, lost creature."

The Chinese proverb speaks of two *good* men: one is *dead,* the other unborn.

All mankind is in need of God's salvation.

The gospel of Luke continues to tell of a woman who had ten pieces of silver. Of the ten pieces, the woman lost one. The coin couldn't call out its location. It was totally helpless. But the woman sought the lost coin. The Scripture says, "And when she hath found it, she calleth her friends and her neighbors together, saying, Rejoice with me; for I have found the piece which I had lost" (Lk 15:9).

The gospel of Luke continues by giving an account of a wayward son. The rebellious, lost son is a picture of mankind, lost and apart from God. The father in this parable is a picture of the heavenly Father, seeking the departed. Eventually, we are told, the son repented and started back.

"And he arose, and came to his father. But when he was yet a great way off, his father saw him, and had compassion, and ran, and fell on his neck, and kissed him. And the son said unto him, Father, I have sinned against heaven, and in thy sight, and am no more worthy to be called thy son. But the father said to his servants, Bring forth the best robe, and put it on him; and put a ring on his hand, and shoes on his feet. And bring the fatted calf, and kill it; and let us eat, and be merry. For this, my son, was dead, and is alive again; he was lost, and is found. And they began to be merry" (Lk 15:20-24).

Have you been found by God?

In his poem "Credo," Edwin Arlington Robinson describes his flight. He writes, "I cannot find my way; there's not a glimmer, not a call in all the black heavens anywhere." Here he expresses something of the lostness of mankind. Man is lost, afraid, lonely, and helpless. Robinson also said, "The world is like a kindergarten where the inhabitants are like children trying to spell God with the wrong blocks."

Francis Thompson wrote a great poem entitled, "The

Hound of Heaven," in which he pictures God chasing man. The hound suggests speed, grace, and instancy. The poet writes,

> I fled Him, down the nights and down the days;
>   I fled Him down the arches of the years;
> I fled Him down the labyrinthine ways
>   Of my own mind; and in the midst of tears
> I hid from Him, and under running laughter.
> From those strong Feet that followed, followed after.

My friend, God loves you! God is seeking you! God is pursuing you! And you cannot ultimately escape.

This is the world's greatest manhunt. God in pursuit of needy people. He is calling, Where are you? Why are you afraid? Why are you running?

As a little child I wandered off from my parents and became lost in the forest. While it was light I was undisturbed; but soon darkness came, and I was terrified. After a while, I heard my father's distant voice calling, "Where are you?" My father had found me, and soon I would be safe in his strong arms.

In John 14 we read, "And where I go ye know, and the way ye know. Thomas saith unto him, Lord, we know not where thou goest; and how can we know the way? Jesus saith unto him, I am the way, the truth, and the life; no man cometh unto the Father, but by me" (vv. 4-6).

Will you, in faith, receive Jesus Christ right now?

How to Start Living All Over Again

RECENTLY, while waiting to board a plane, I became engaged in conversation with a businessman and his wife. After watching several jets shoot into the murky darkness, the young woman remarked, "I wish I could vanish into space just like that plane and start life all over again."

She was a young and attractive woman, a woman of wealth and position; and yet her life was filled with emptiness and regret.

Why did she want to vanish? Why did she want to escape? Because the ugly hand of the past was spoiling the present. She wanted a new start in life.

There are many people today who echo these words of despair. Millions are driven by this haunting desire.

Several months ago one of our national news magazines featured an article on Americans who were emigrating to Australia. Some of the modern "pilgrims" who were interviewed indicated they were naturally daring and that they were seeking excitement and adventure.

Most of those going, however, expressed a desire to change their environment. Distressed by rising crime rates, social unrest, and the soaring cost of living in America, they wanted to "get away from it all." They wanted to start life over again.

Have you ever wanted to get away from it all? Have you ever wondered what it would be like to have a new start in life?

Some people only wish to escape. Others find something to help them escape. Many try to drink away their gloom. Some seek release through drugs or sex. Others create their own private fantasies — anything to help them forget the misery of their everyday existence.

In A.D. 1212, Europe witnessed an amazing event. The spirit of the Crusades charmed a young boy named Stephen, who took up a cross and started marching. Soon, hundreds of children, tired of tending sheep and working in the fields, started to follow him. Stephen promised to lead them over the mountains and through the seas to God. Carrying their wooden crosses, they sang while they marched down the hills and valleys of Italy. They came — by the thousands they came — with but one chorus on their lips, "We are going to God."

Historians tell us that the real reason for this Children's Crusade was that these young people were trying to escape from the realities of their world. No doubt, this is why many children were inspired by Stephen's call to adventure.

But did they escape? Sadly, the answer is no. When they came to Genoa and Venice, they were met by every kind of evil. Slave traders carried them off to Egypt; many became ill and died, while others were robbed and molested. Some turned back, without a cross, without a song. All were disillusioned and discouraged.

Why do people want a new start? Why are people seeking for a way to escape? Why? Allow me to suggest three reasons for being dissatisfied with life on the natural plane, and follow this with one glorious alternative.

Life on the natural plane is incomplete morally, intellectually, and physically. We know what is good. We know what we would like to have; and yet we see evil, war, and deception on every side. Daily we are confronted with corruption in government, dishonesty in business, and cheating in marriage. Our faith in mankind is shattered.

Man once knew what is good, what is true and right; but he has fallen from this knowledge. He has become cynical. Our society has become morally bankrupt, and we are unable to cope with the evil that surrounds us.

Never forget, my friend, life on the natural plane is incomplete. And until a man comes to God, he is racked by emptiness within his soul.

Life on the natural plane is disappointing. A. B. Bragdon wrote,

> Alas how scant the sheaves for all the trouble,
> The toil, the pain and the resolve sublime —
> A few full ears; the rest but weeds and stubble,
> And withered, wildflowers plucked before their time.

To many, life is one continual disappointment. Coningsby said, "Youth is a blunder; manhood a struggle; old age a regret."

Shakespeare pictured the shortness and futility of life in his play *MacBeth*:

> Out, out brief candle!
> Life's but a walking shadow; a poor player
> That struts and frets his hour upon the stage
>   and then is heard no more,
> It is a tale told by an idiot, full of sound and
>   fury, signifying nothing.

Regardless of who we are or how much of the world's wealth we possess, life on the natural plane can be disappointing.

Recently, the teenage grandson of billionaire industrialist Cyrus Eaton ran away for his Cleveland home. When located by authorities in Tennessee and asked why he did such a thing, he replied, "I'm not happy; I want to start a new life."

Life on the natural plane is sinful. Men and women want to live above the downward pull, but they cannot. They want to fly above, but they have no wings.

In 1 Corinthians 2:14 we read, "The natural man receiveth not the things of the Spirit of God; for they are foolishness unto him, neither can he know them, because they are spiritually discerned."

By himself, man finds it impossible to overcome the weight of sin.

In my counseling over the years, I have found that most people do not have to be convinced of their sin. Our conscience condemns us. God's Word plainly states our condition: "All we like sheep have gone astray; we have turned every one to his own way." We cannot even meet our own standards of conduct, let alone the standards that God has set.

The apostle Paul said, "What I would, that do I not."

The prophet Isaiah lamented, "Woe is me! For I am undone, because I am a man of unclean lips."

Job, an upright and moral man, confessed, "I am vile."

The English poet, Coleridge said, "We have all sinned, some more, some less."

Life on the natural plane is sinful and self-centered. Without Jesus Christ there is lack of purpose. Without Jesus Christ there is fear and insecurity. Without Jesus Christ there is no inner peace. There is loneliness; there is a vacuum.

Life on the natural plane can be changed. There is an answer to sin. There is an answer to this disappointment and emptiness. You can have a new start today!

Paul said, "If any man be in Christ, he is a new creation; old things are passed away; behold, all things are become new."

A new start is not to be found in some other place. Many people seem to think they can gain a new start by moving to a new area. Young people run away from home. Businessmen quit their jobs and seek new employment. Couples leave the community when one of the partners has been found to be unfaithful.

The chance for a new start is not found in a new job, or a new home, or even in a new environment. With God's power and forgiveness, you can have a new start right where you are.

But what is it like to experience a new start in Jesus Christ, to experience a change within yourself, to experience God's life?

Martin Luther described his experience this way: "When by the Spirit of God, I understood these words, 'The just shall live by faith,' I felt born again like a new man; I entered through the open doors into the very paradise of God!"

Someone else, describing his new life in Christ, said, "Everything seems new — the Bible, my friends, my love for others, even Sunday itself. I have a new desire for spiritual things, a desire to know more about God and His church."

We must begin by acknowledging that we need God's help, God's power, and God's life. Dead things cannot grow; and without Christ, we are spiritually dead. We are powerless and defeated.

Have you ever acknowledged that Jesus Christ can meet your need? This could be your chance for a new start.

Napoleon believed that the fate of every battle was decided in the space of five minutes. All his maneuvering and planning led to that strategic moment of crisis, the moment of action and decision.

So with you, my friend. Your future, your eternal welfare is decided in but a few moments of decision.

Shakespeare wrote,

> There is a tide in the affairs of men,
> Which taken at the flood, leads on to fortune;
> Omitted, all the voyage of their life
> Is bound in shallows and in miseries.

You are what you are because of how you react in the moments of decision.

How to Start Living All Over Again

Centuries ago, Kadesh-Barnea, located on the southern border of the promised land, was the place of decision for God's people, Israel. The people were ready to possess the land that God had promised to them. Twelve spies had been sent out to view the land and bring back a report. Ten of those sent out returned saying, "It can't be done. The enemy is too strong; the cities are fortified; the land is impenetrable." Only two of the twelve, Caleb and Joshua, reported, "We can take the land."

Because of fear and doubt, the children of Israel failed to enter the promised land. For forty more years they wandered in the wilderness, forty more long years before their children were able to realize the blessings God had prepared for them. This was the world's longest funeral march, as the punishment for their unbelief was death.

The children of Israel missed their chance. They failed in their strategic moment of decision. My friend, there is a Kadesh-Barnea in every life. There is a moment of decision facing you right now. Will you continue to hold back, or will you allow Jesus Christ to transform your life, to give you a new start?

J. B. Phillips has translated 2 Corinthians 5:17, "If a man is in Christ he becomes a new person altogether — the past is finished and gone, everything has become fresh and new."

My friend, you can have a new start today. Acknowledge Jesus Christ as your Saviour and receive Him right now!

How to Live Above Worry

WOULD YOU LIKE a solid formula for solving worry situations?
An approach you can start using this very day?
Do you know how to live a day at a time?

LIVE ONE DAY AT A TIME

In the spring of 1871, a young man picked up a book and read twenty-one words that absolutely changed his life. The young man was a medical student at the Montreal General Hospital. He was worried about final examinations. Larger worries also bothered him. He was troubled about what he should do with his life, where he should establish his medical practice, and how he would build it.

The twenty-one words that changed this man's life were written by Thomas Carlyle. The man who was challenged was William Osler, a founder of John Hopkins School of Medicine. These are the twenty-one words:

> Our main business is not to see
> What lies dimly at a distance, but
> To do what lies clearly at hand.

This truth is taught in what we usually call the Lord's Prayer. Jesus prayed, "Give us this day our daily bread" (Mt 6:11). Notice the words "this day." The prayer asks for today's bread only. It does not complain about yesterday's bread. It does not worry about the bread for the next week or next month. The request focuses on *this day*.

Today's bread is the only bread we can possibly eat. This is exactly what the Bible teaches. In Matthew 6:34 we read,

How to Live Above Worry

"Be, therefore, not anxious about tomorrow: for the morrow shall take thought for the things of itself. Sufficient unto the day is its own evil." Matthew is telling us to live one day at a time. If we do our best each day for God's glory, we will automatically be prepared for tomorrow and the future.

Jesus Christ is saying, "Don't worry about tomorrow."

Robert Burdette wrote, "There are two days in the week about which I never worry. Two carefree days, kept sacredly free from fear and apprehension. One of these days is yesterday — and the other day I do not worry about is tomorrow." Not many people follow this advice, and therefore our age has become the age of worry.

Hypertension winds us up and also wears us down. "Died of worry" or "Felled by fretting" could be written on thousands of tombstones. Dr. Alexis Carroll said, "People who do not know how to fight worry, die young."

Worry is a leading ailment in our world, and unfortunately it is contagious. It is easily caught!

WHAT IS WORRY?

George Washington Lyon once said, "Worry is the interest paid by those who borrow trouble."

Our English word *worry* comes from the Greek word *merimnao*. It is a combination of two words, *merizo* meaning "to divide," and *nous* meaning "mind." Worry therefore means "to divide the mind."

We see this discussed in James 1:8, "A double-minded man is unstable in all his ways." In other words, a man troubled by worry is divided emotionally, mentally, and spiritually.

Charles Haddon Spurgeon, the great nineteenth-century London minister, relates how he worried for weeks before a speaking engagement, even to the extent of hoping he would break a leg before the particular occasion. The result was that when he entered the pulpit, he was exhausted from worry.

Then Spurgeon faced up to the situation. He asked, "What is the worst thing that could happen to me during my sermon?" Whatever it was, he decided, the heavens would not fall. He recognized that he had been magnifying his fears abnormally. When he faced his worries for what they were, he relaxed, simply because his mind was no longer divided.

It might be wise to make a list of what worries you. As you list the various items you will discover that many are vague and really quite unnecessary.

Worry leads to loss of power to will. When we worry we become so divided that it is difficult to act in a single direction. Business and professional men often become so divided and frustrated by the problems confronting them, that they reach the point where they are unable to make even the smallest decision.

WORRY IS A SIN

My friend, worry is an enemy! It is an enemy to your future; yes, an enemy to your health and to your family. Let me carry this thought a step further. Worry is not only a divider of the mind, but beyond this, worry is sinful.

When a believer in Christ worries, he accuses God of falsehood. The Bible says in Romans 8:28, "And we know that all things work together for good to them that love God." Worry says, "That's a lie." The apostle Paul wrote, "I can do all things through Christ, who strengtheneth me" (Phil 4:13). Worry whines, "Are you going to believe that?" God says in Hebrews 13:5, "I will never leave thee, nor forsake thee." Worry blasphemes, "Untrue! Pure foolishness!" Christ says in Matthew 6:33, "Seek ye first the kingdom of God, and his righteousness, and all these things shall be added unto you." Worry retorts, "I don't believe you, Creator of the universe."

When you worry, you are slapping God in the face with the glove of disbelief. Worry is outright hypocrisy; it claims faith in God while, at the same time, worry doubts God's truthfulness. In 1 John 5:10 we read, "He that believeth not God hath made him a liar."

Worry is also a sin because it is harmful to the human body, the temple of God. It is a medical fact that worried people have more accidents resulting in fractures than those who are single-minded.

In Gen. Ulysses S. Grant's memoirs he tells how he was dizzy and could not see well because of violent headaches. His entire body ached. The following morning a horseman galloped up to him with a note of surrender from Gen. Robert E. Lee. Grant said, "I was instantly cured when I saw the contents of the note. Every pain immediately left me; even my headache." Obviously Grant was sick from worry. Worry hurts the human body.

Just suppose a group of vandals broke into your local church, smashed stained glass windows, splintered pews, stained the carpet. You would be outraged and rightly so. Desecrating the house of God is a despicable sin.

Yet it is far more tragic to desecrate your body, God's temple, through worry. Paul asks in 1 Corinthians 3:16, "Know ye not that ye are the temple of God, and that the Spirit of God dwelleth in you?" My friend, be careful how you treat your body. Worry is harmful. In fact, worry is sinful.

THE CURE FOR WORRY

1. *Try prayer.* In Luke 18:1 we read, "Men ought always to pray, and not to faint." Prayer is one of God's cures for caving in. Let's do what that great hymn suggests, "Take it to the Lord in prayer."

On Sunday, August 15, 1971 the *New York Times* carried

a front-page feature story written by John McCandlish Phillips, entitled "Family Portraits of Three Astronauts."

After interviewing the Scott and Irwin families of the Apollo 15 mission, Phillips wrote, "They are buoyed by strong, active religious beliefs, often of the Bible-toting, go-to-meeting kind, and they profess to lean as much on prayer as in technology when one of their members goes off to the moon." Yes, try prayer.

2. *Try rejoicing.* The New Testament book of Phillippians suggests, "Rejoice in the Lord always; and again I say, Rejoice" (Phil 4:4). You may say, "I'm not in a rejoicing mood. I just don't feel like rejoicing." Most people let their circumstances control them. The verb in Phillippians 4:4 is the imperative present. It is mandatory. "Keep on praising the Lord." Paul does not say, "If you are so inclined, please let me suggest that you rejoice." No, he was led of the Holy Spirit to write, "Keep on rejoicing in the Lord always."

David said in Psalm 34:1, "I will bless the Lord at all times; his praise shall continually be in my mouth."

David did not lead a sheltered life. God did not transport him about in a transparent plastic shell. Adonijah broke his heart. Absalom betrayed him. Earlier, Saul had hounded him.

But the pattern of David's life was praise. He chose happiness. Psalm 33:1 states, "Rejoice in the Lord, O ye righteous; for praise is befitting to the upright." Praise is attractive.

Have you ever stopped to think that a thermometer Christian registers the temperature that surrounds him? A thermostat Christian establishes the temperature.

3. *Try trusting.* Psalm 37 tells us not to fret but to trust. "Trust in the Lord, and do good" (Ps 37:3).

My third suggestion for worry is total trust in Jesus Christ. Fretting creates friction but no power. Fretting only heats the axle but does not generate speed. Notice again the words of Jesus in the text of Matthew 6. If God cares for the birds of the air and the flowers of the field, will He not take care of you? Worry in a sense is a form of atheism; it is a denial of God's concern and Christ's intercessory work. Matthew reminds us that Solomon, in all of his wealth, was not dressed like one of these wild flowers. Even the costliest silk has microscopic flaws in it, but not God's lilies of the field. If you trust you will not worry.

4. *Try work.* Psalm 37 suggests, "Trust in the LORD, and do good." One of the best cures for worry is work. "It is not work that kills men," wrote Henry Ward Beecher. "It is worry. Work is healthy. . . . Worry is rust upon the blade." Matthew verifies this: "But seek ye first the kingdom of God, and his righteousness, and all these things shall be added unto you." If we put the Lord and His work first, He will add to us all that is necessary in life.

5. *Try counting your blessings.* Another suggestion for overcoming worry is to list your blessings.

Someone has written, "I had the blues because I had no shoes; till upon the street I met a man who had no feet."

Count your blessings today. Look around you. Thank God for your loved ones, perhaps a husband or wife, parents, children, your job, your country, your health, your possessions, your church fellowship, the Word of God, your personal faith in Jesus Christ.

Recall Psalm 139:17. "How precious also are thy thoughts unto me, O God! How great is the sum of them!" In the next verse the psalmist said, "If I should count them, they are more in number than the sand." Have you tried to count your blessings?

Friend, I want to tell you that if your basic needs have not been met in Jesus Christ, you *do* have something to worry about. If you do not have peace with the Creator and Redeemer of the universe, you *have* cause for anxiety. But there is hope; there is reason for rejoicing. Christ wants to forgive you.

A starving man has one interest — food. A thirsty man has one interest — water. A person without Jesus Christ, whether he knows it or not, needs one thing — forgiveness.

Jesus said when He was here on this earth, "I am the way, the truth, and the life; no man cometh unto the Father, but by me" (Jn 14:6).

Do you want to rid yourself of anxiety? Do you want to win out over worry? Stop seeking the trivial; *seek Jesus Christ*. Do not continue to major in the minor, the trivia of life. View life from God's perspective through the lens of eternity. Concern yourself with the kingdom of God. J. B. Phillips paraphrased Matthew 6:33 in this way: "Set your heart on his kingdom and his goodness, and all these things will come to you as a matter of course."

A final suggestion. Get your eyes *off yourself*. Focus them on the Saviour and upon *others*. Remember the word that Paul wrote to the congregation of Christians in Philippi, "Look not every man on his own things, but every man also on the things of others" (Phil 2:4).

My friend, commit yourself 100 percent to Jesus Christ. He will deliver you from a divided mind.